The Joys of Hashing

Hash Table Programming with C

Second Edition

Thomas Mailund

Apress®

The Joys of Hashing: Hash Table Programming with C, Second Edition

Thomas Mailund
Aarhus N, Denmark

ISBN-13 (pbk): 979-8-8688-0825-8   ISBN-13 (electronic): 979-8-8688-0826-5
https://doi.org/10.1007/979-8-8688-0826-5

Managing Director, Apress Media LLC: Welmoed Spahr
Acquisitions Editor: Melissa Duffy
Development Editor: James Markham
Coordinating Editor: Gryffin Winkler
Copy Editor: Kezia Endsley

Cover designed by eStudioCalamar

Cover image designed by Freepik (www.freepik.com)

Distributed to the book trade worldwide by Apress Media, LLC, 1 New York Plaza, New York, NY 10004, U.S.A. Phone 1-800-SPRINGER, fax (201) 348-4505, e-mail orders-ny@springer-sbm.com, or visit www.springeronline.com. Apress Media, LLC is a California LLC and the sole member (owner) is Springer Science + Business Media Finance Inc (SSBM Finance Inc). SSBM Finance Inc is a **Delaware** corporation.

For information on translations, please e-mail booktranslations@springernature.com; for reprint, paperback, or audio rights, please e-mail bookpermissions@springernature.com.

Apress titles may be purchased in bulk for academic, corporate, or promotional use. eBook versions and licenses are also available for most titles. For more information, reference our Print and eBook Bulk Sales web page at http://www.apress.com/bulk-sales.

Any source code or other supplementary material referenced by the author in this book is available to readers on GitHub (https://github.com/Apress). For more detailed information, please visit https://www.apress.com/gp/services/source-code.

If disposing of this product, please recycle the paper

Table of Contents

About the Author vii

About the Technical Reviewer ix

Acknowledgments xi

Chapter 1: Introduction...1

Chapter 2: Hash Keys, Indices, and Collisions 7

Mapping from Keys to Indices to Bins 14

Hash table operations 18

    Collision risk 21

Conclusion 28

Chapter 3: Collision Resolution, Load Factor, and Performance........29

Chaining 29

    Linked Lists 30

    Chained Hashing Collision Resolution 35

Open Addressing 38

    Probing Strategies 42

Load and Performance... 46

    Theoretical Runtime Performance... 46

Experiments 54

Conclusion 59

Chapter 4: Resizing 61

Amortizing Resizing Costs 62

Resizing Chained Hash Tables 70

Resizing Open Addressing Hash Tables 74

Theoretical Considerations for Choosing the Load Factor 80

Experiments 84

Resizing When Table Sizes Are Not Powers of Two 89

Dynamic Resizing...99

Chapter 5: Adding Application Keys and Values..................115

Generating Hash Sets 117

    Generic Lists..119

    Generating a Hash Set...127

Hash Maps 134

    Key and Value Types..136

    Hash Map Definition 137

    Creating and Resizing a Table 140

    Freeing Tables 142

    Lookup...144

    Adding and Deleting 146

Conclusions..150

Chapter 6: Heuristic Hash Functions 151

What Makes a Good Hash Function? 153

Hashing Computer Words...155

    Additive Hashing...157

    Rotating Hashing 159

    One-at-a-Time Hashing 163

    Jenkins Hashing 171

Hashing Strings of Bytes..175

Chapter 7: Universal Hashing **183**

Uniformly Distributed Keys 184

Universal Hashing 185

Stronger Universal Families 186

    Binning Hash Keys..187

    Collision Resolution Strategies 189

Constructing Universal Families 190

    Nearly Universal Families 190

    Polynomial Construction for k-Independent Families 191

    Tabulation Hashing 193

    Performance Comparison..197

Re-hashing..201

Chapter 8: Conclusions...**211**

Index...**213**

About the Author

Thomas Mailund is a former associate professor in bioinformatics at Aarhus University, Denmark, and currently a senior software architect at the quantum computing company Kvantify. He has a background in math and computer science, including experience programming and teaching in the C and R programming languages. For the last decade, his main focus has been on genetics and evolutionary studies, particularly comparative genomics, speciation, and gene flow between emerging species.

About the Technical Reviewer

 **Megan J. Hirni** currently teaches and conducts research at the University of Missouri-Columbia, focusing on statistical methodology applied in health, social sciences, and education. Apart from her passion for coding, Megan enjoys meeting new people and exploring diverse research disciplines.

Acknowledgments

I am very grateful to Rasmus Pagh for his comments on the manuscript, for suggestions on topics to add, and for correcting me when I was imprecise or downright wrong. I am also grateful to Anders Halager for many discussions about implementation details and bit-fiddling. I am also grateful to Shiella Balbutin for proofreading the book.

CHAPTER 1

Introduction

This book is an introduction to the *hash table* data structure. When implemented and used appropriately, hash tables are exceptionally efficient data structures for representing sets and lookup tables. They provide constant time, low overhead, insertion, deletion, and lookup. This book assumes you are familiar with programming and the C programming language. The theoretical parts of the book also assume some familiarity with probability theory and algorithmic theory, but nothing beyond what you would learn in an introductory course.

Hash tables are constructed from two fundamental ideas: reducing application keys to a *hash key*—a number ranging from 0 to some $N - 1$—and mapping that number into a smaller range from 0 to $m - 1$, $m \ll N$. You can use the small range to index into an array with constant time access. Both ideas are simple, but how they are implemented in practice affects the efficiency of hash tables.

Consider Figure 1-1, which illustrates the main components of storing values in a hash table. Potentially complex application values are mapped to *hash keys*, which are integer values in a range of size N, usually 0 to $N - 1$. In the figure, $N = 64$. Doing this simplifies the representation of the values. You now only have integers as keys, and if N is small, you can store the integers in an array of size N. You use their hash keys as their index into the array. However, if N is large, this is not feasible. If, for example, the space of hash keys is 32-bit integers, then $N = 4,294,967,295$; slightly more than four billion. An array of bytes of this size would take up more than 4GB of space. You would need between four and eight times as much memory to store pointers or integers, for example, which are still simple objects. It is impractical to use this size of an array to store some application keys.

Even if N is considerably smaller than four-byte words, if you plan to store $n \ll N$ keys, you waste a lot of space to have the array. Since this array needs to be allocated and initialized, merely creating it will cost you $O(N)$. Even if you get constant time insertion and deletion into such an array, the cost of producing it can easily swamp the time your algorithm will spend while using the array. If you want an efficient table, you should be able to initialize it and use it to insert or delete n keys, all in time $O(n)$. Therefore, N should be in $O(n)$.

The typical solution is to keep N large, but include a second step that reduces the hash key range to a smaller bin-range of size m with $m \in O(n)$—this example uses $m = 8$. If you keep m small (i.e., in $O(n)$), you can allocate and initialize it in linear time and get any bin in it in constant time. To insert, check, or delete an element in the table, you map the application value to its hash key and then map the hash key to a bin index.

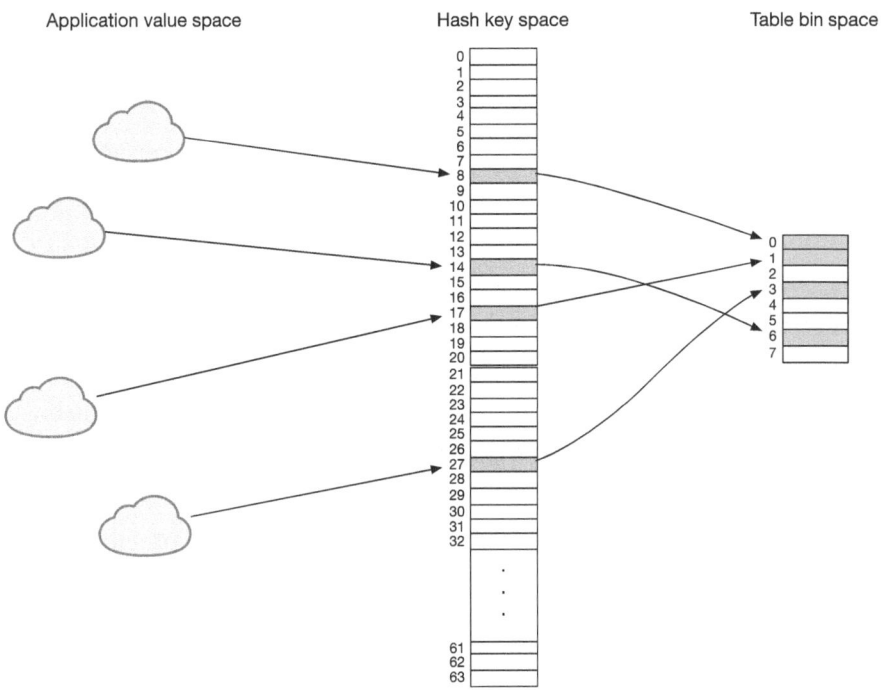

Figure 1-1. *Value maps to hash keys that then maps to table bins*

You can reduce values to bin indices in two steps. The first step, mapping data from your application domain to a number, is program-specific and cannot be part of a general hash table implementation.[1] Moving from large integer intervals to smaller, however, can be implemented as part of the hash table. If you resize the table to adapt it to the number of keys you store, you need to change m. You do not want the application programmer to provide separate functions for each m. You can

---

[1] In some textbooks, you will see the hashing step and the binning step combined, called *hashing*. Then, you have a single function that maps application-specific keys directly to bins. I prefer to consider this as two or three separate functions, and it is usually implemented as such.

think of the hash key space, $[N] = [0, ..., N - 1]$, as the interface between the application and the data structure. The hash table itself can map from this space to indices in an array, $[m] = [0, ..., m - 1]$.

The primary responsibility of the first step is to reduce potentially complicated application values into simpler hash keys. For example, to map application-relevant information like positions on a board game or connections in a network down to integers. These integers can then be handled by the hash table data structure. The second responsibility of the function is to make the hash keys uniformly distributed in the range $[N]$. The binning strategy for mapping hash keys to bins assumes that the hash keys are uniformly distributed to distribute keys evenly into bins. If this is violated, the data structure does not guarantee (expected) constant time operations. Here, you can add a third step between the two previous that maps from $[N] \rightarrow [N]$ and scrambles the application hash keys to hash keys with a better distribution. See Figure 1-2. These functions can be application-independent and part of a hash table library.

Chapters 6 and 7 return to these functions. Having a middle step does not eliminate the need for application hash functions. You still need to map complex data into integers. The middle step only alleviates the need for an even distribution of keys. The map from application keys to hash keys still has some responsibility for this, though. If it maps different data to the same hash keys, the middle step cannot do anything but map the same input to the same output.

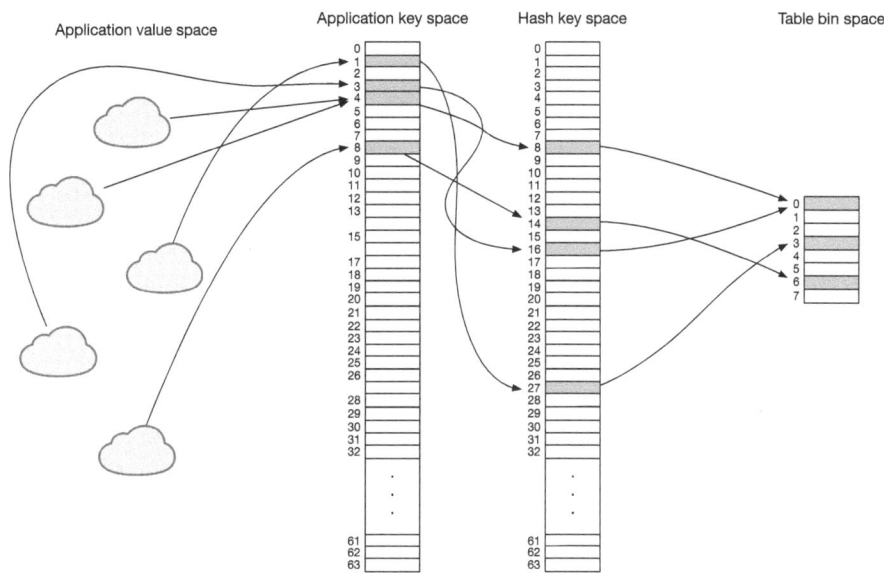

Figure 1-2. *If the application maps values to keys, but they are not uniformly distributed, then a hashing step between the application and the binning can be added*

Strictly speaking, you do not need the distribution of hash keys to be uniform as long as the likelihood of two different values mapping to the same key is improbable. The goal is to have uniformly distributed hash keys, which are easiest to work with when analyzing theoretical performance. The runtime results in Chapter 3 assume this, and therefore, you can as well. Chapter 7 considers techniques for achieving similar results without the assumption.

The book is primarily about implementing the hash table data structure and only secondarily about hash functions. When implementing hash tables, the concerns are these: given hash keys with application values attached to them, how do you represent the data so that you can update and query tables in constant time? The fundamental idea is, of course, to reduce hash keys to bins and then use an array of bins containing values. In the purest form, you can store your data values

5

directly in the array at the index that the hash and binning functions provide. Still, if m is relatively small compared to the number of data values, you are likely to have *collisions*, which are cases where two hash keys map to the same bin. Although different values are unlikely to hash to the same key in the range $[N]$, this does not mean that collisions are unlikely in the range $[m]$ if m is smaller than N (and as the number of keys you insert in the table, n, approaches m, collisions are guaranteed). Dealing with collisions is a crucial aspect of implementing hash tables and a topic that's covered in a sizeable portion of this book.

CHAPTER 2

Hash Keys, Indices, and Collisions

As mentioned in the introduction, this book is primarily about implementing hash tables and not hash functions. So, to simplify the exposition, I initially assume that the data values you store in tables are simply hash keys. Chapter 5 addresses the changes you have to make to store application data together with keys, but for most of the theory of hash tables, you only need to consider hash keys. Everywhere else, you will view additional data as black box data and just store their keys.

While the code snippets cover all that you need to implement the concepts in this chapter, you cannot easily compile them from the book, but you can download the complete code listings from `https://github.com/mailund/JoyChapter2`. I did not include the necessary header files in the source code snippets throughout the book, but you can access them in the repository links found at the beginning of each chapter.

I assume that the keys are uniformly distributed in the interval $[N] = [0, ..., N-1]$, where N is the maximum `unsigned int`, and consider the most straightforward hash table I can imagine. It consists of an array where you can store keys and a number holding the size of the table, m. To be able to map from the range $[N]$ to the range $[m]$, you need to remember m, and that is why you store it. If you always had the same table size, you wouldn't even need that, and a hash table would be an array. But you will allow for different table sizes (when you get to Chapter 4), so you need to store the number m in the variable size using the following structure:

```
struct bin { ... };
struct hash_table {
  struct bin *table;
  unsigned int size;
};
```

If your bins are just an array of hash keys with no further information, you have an interesting problem. If you find a key k in the bin where you expect to find k, does that mean it is actually there? After all, an array is usually uninitialized memory, so it *could* happen that k was there by pure chance. Admittedly, this is extremely unlikely to happen, and I wouldn't worry about it happening in real life if the space of keys is large, but we might as well consider and deal with the issue.

If the bits you have in a bin are precisely the bits you have for hash keys, there is little that you can do about it. You need at least one bit of information to indicate whether an array entry is initialized. There are clever ways of representing such information without putting it in bins, but that puts the extra information elsewhere, in auxiliary data structures. You need a simple table here, so I do not want to go there, now or ever.

A simple solution is to add one bit of information to each bin:

```
struct bin {
  int is_free : 1;
  unsigned int key;
};

struct hash_table {
  struct bin *table;
  unsigned int size;
};
```

That increases the size of the bins and leaves enough bits for the keys and the initialization indicator. Unfortunately, even though you only ask for one bit for the is_free flag, you can potentially get a lot more. The struct bin has to contain enough memory for both is_free and key, but your computer does not allocate memory in bit-sized chunks, so the size must be rounded up. Furthermore, the memory alignment of various types will usually result in even more rounding up. If your computer stores integers as four bytes, it might also demand that all integers are at offsets that are multiples of fours, and when it sees a struct like this, it will set aside two integers per struct bin. So, by adding one bit, you have doubled the bin size.

You should rarely worry about this, but it can be wasteful. Instead, you could remove one bit from the hash keys, using, for example, 31 bits for keys, and then one bit for is_free, packing both neatly into a 32-bit integer. In practice, there is not much difference between 31-bit and 32-bit keys, but you have just halved the space of keys, which also feels a bit dramatic. So I won't go there, especially because cutting the key space in half is unnecessary to represent whether a bin is initialized or not. You could reserve a unique key value to indicate that and require that no one uses that hash key for anything else. Zero, for example. Then bins can be unsigned int, and you don't need extra space.

```
#define RESERVED_KEY ((unsigned int)0)
struct hash_table {
  unsigned int size;
  unsigned int *bins;
};
```

For the user who has to generate hash keys, avoiding a reserved key is a potential problem, but if that is the case, the previous solution is an adequate fallback choice. In any case, once you get to more complicated tables, you will need more data in bins in any case, and then the extra is_free bit will be free, or you will need more special values for reserved keys, and you will need to deal with these anyway. So, I go with the two cases without complicating it further, and later in the book, you will see more variations on both themes.

A function for allocating a table can then look like this for the variant with struct bin:

```
struct hash_table *
new_table(unsigned int size)
{
  // Allocate table and bins
  struct hash_table *table = malloc(sizeof *table);
  table->size = size;
  table->bins = malloc(size * sizeof *table->bins);

  // Set all bins to free
  struct bin *beg = table->bins, *end = beg + size;
  for (struct bin *bin = beg; bin != end; bin++) {
    bin->is_free = true;
  }

  return table;
}
```

And it can look like this for the variant with a reserved key:

```
struct hash_table *
new_table(unsigned int size)
{
  // Allocate table and bins
  struct hash_table *table = malloc(sizeof *table);
  table->bins = malloc(size * sizeof *table->bins);

  // Initialize the bins with the reserved key
  unsigned int *beg = table->bins, *end = beg + size;
```

```
  for (unsigned int *bin = beg; bin != end; bin++) {
    *bin = RESERVED_KEY;
  }

  return table;
}
```

They are pretty similar. In both cases, you allocate the hash_table structure and then allocate the bins, after which you iterate through all the bins to initialize them.

I haven't dealt with allocation errors (malloc() returning NULL) in either function. You could easily do it here. For example, the "reserved key" initialization could look like this:

```
struct hash_table *
new_table(unsigned int size)
{
  // Allocate table and bins
  struct hash_table *table = malloc(sizeof *table);
  unsigned int *bins = malloc(size * sizeof *bins);
  if (!table || !bins) goto error;

  *table = (struct hash_table){.size = size, .bins = bins};

  unsigned int *beg = table->bins, *end = beg + size;
  for (unsigned int *bin = beg; bin != end; bin++) {
    *bin = RESERVED_KEY;
  }

  return table;

error:
  free(table);
  free(bins);
  return NULL;
}
```

However, once you start resizing tables in Chapter 4, dealing with allocation errors gets far more complicated. Especially when every allocation error potentially has to propagate out from deeply nested function calls, and C doesn't have any convenient mechanism for error propagation. While I believe that learning how to handle allocation errors is important, my attempts at doing that for the more complicated code you will see in that chapter overshadowed the hash-table lessons, and the book is about hash tables and not error handling in C. That may be an exciting topic for a later book, but it will not be this one. What I am saying is that I won't be handling `malloc()` errors in the book. If you want, pretend that my `malloc()` is a variant that calls `exit()` if it fails.

One more thing I want to say about memory allocation is this: if you can pack your data into fewer allocations, it is easier to work with. You could have done that by putting the bins in a "flexible array member" as so:

```
struct hash_table {
  unsigned int size;
  struct bin bins[];  // flexible array member
};
```

A flexible array member is an array you declare at the end of a `struct` without specifying its length. If you have such a member, you can allocate the hash_table and the bins in a single call to `malloc()`:

```
struct hash_table *
new_table(unsigned int size)
{
  // Allocate table and bins
  struct hash_table *table =
    malloc(sizeof *table + size * sizeof *table->bins);

  if (table) {
    table->size = size;
    struct bin *beg = table->bins, *end = beg + size;
```

```
    for (struct bin *bin = beg; bin != end; bin++) {
      bin->is_free = true;
    }
  }

  return table;
}
```

The trick is to allocate enough memory in the malloc() call for both the struct and the elements you want to put in the array. Here I do that by simply adding the size of the struct to the size of the bins array. Depending on the memory layout of the struct members, this *might* be slightly more than I need, and I could instead add the offset of the array to the size of the array, but the difference hardly matters.

I don't use a flexible array member in this book, and it is for the same reason that I don't include allocation error handling. While the flexible array member is often helpful, it can get complicated if you need to reallocate memory to grow or shrink your tables. Suppose you allocate one block of memory for the table plus the bins. In that case, you cannot easily add or remove bins later because every pointer to the table has to be updated to point to the newly allocated version. If you have a pointer to a table, and it has a pointer to its bins, you can update the bins pointer once, and everyone will have access to it. Because of this, I allocate bins separately from the hash_table structure.

To free a table's memory again, you need to free both the table structure and the bins array. For the two first versions, where you allocated the bins separately, it looks like this:

```
void
delete_table(struct hash_table *table)
{
  free(table->bins);
  free(table);
}
```

For the flexible array member version, you can write the function as:

```
void
delete_table(struct hash_table *table)
{
  free(table);
}
```

or just use `free()`.

Anyway, you have some options for constructing and deleting a hash table. Now, you need to implement some operations on it. The operations for hash tables are the insertion and deletion of keys and queries to test if a table holds a given key. You can use this interface for the operations:

```
void insert_key   (struct hash_table *table, unsigned int key);
bool contains_key (struct hash_table *table, unsigned int key);
void delete_key   (struct hash_table *table, unsigned int key);
```

All three will need a way to get a bin from a hash key, and the way to do this is the same for all three operations, so let's handle that first.

Mapping from Keys to Indices to Bins

When you have to map a hash key from [N] down to the range of the indices in the array, [m], the most straightforward approach is to take the remainder of a division by m, using the modulo operator:

```
static inline unsigned int
hash_bin_index(struct hash_table *table, unsigned int key)
{
  return key % table->size;
}
```

This solution will work for all $m < N$ in the sense that it maps from $[N]$ to $[m]$. However, even if you are lucky enough to have uniformly distributed keys in $[N]$, the golden standard of hash keys, this mapping will not necessarily guarantee that you also get uniformly distributed keys in $[m]$ (which is where it matters, as you shall see shortly).

Using modulo will only map a uniform distribution over $[N]$ to a uniform distribution over $[m]$ when $N \bmod n = 0$; otherwise, some bins will be hit more than others, although only slightly so. If you mapped all the numbers $0...N - 1$ to $[m]$, some lower range of $[m]$ would be hit once more than the remaining if m doesn't divide N exactly. This is usually not worth worrying about since it is as evenly distributed as possible given the two numbers.

Still, I mainly pick m to be such a number in this book for other reasons. Hash keys come in computer words, and their size is almost always powers of two. Picking powers of two for hash table sizes simplifies a few other tasks, so that is what you will do. That this will map uniformly distributed keys to uniformly distributed bins is an added benefit.

That being said, if you read the literature, you will find that most people suggest using hash tables where m is a prime. So what gives? This relates to another issue: you cannot necessarily assume that your hash keys are uniformly distributed. If hash keys have some regular pattern to them, this will affect the performance of your tables. Taking modulo with respect to a prime is a way to alleviate this in some cases.

Assume, for example, that all your hash keys can be written as $h = n \cdot k$. This looks artificial at first glance, but such a pattern is common. If, for example, you want to hash pointers, their lower bits are often zero because different data types often have to sit at specific address offsets. Integers, for example, often have to sit at offsets that are a multiple of four or eight, and that would make integer pointers a type of hash key of the form $n \cdot 4$ or $n \cdot 8$. If your table size m shares a prime factor with h, say $m = m' \cdot k$, then $h \bmod m$ will only take values that are multiples of the shared factor, here k. If $k = 4$ and $m = 8$, you would map 0 mod 8 = 0, 4 mod 8 = 4, 8 mod 8 = 0, 12 mod 8 = 4, 16 mod 8 = 0, and so on. In this example, you would only hit two of the eight bins.

If your table size is prime, you are less likely to share a prime factor with the periodic hash tables. If you do, you would map *everything* into bin 0, which would be bad,[1] but otherwise, you would hit every bin. It would not necessarily be uniform—that would still depend on the distribution of hash keys—but the periodicity would be taken care of.

Sticking to primes has some drawbacks, however. You will often need to resize the tables if the number of keys is not known a priori. You'll look at this in Chapter 4. If you want to stick to primes, you need a table of primes to pick from when growing or shrinking your table. If you instead choose table sizes that are powers of two, it is straightforward to grow and shrink them. You can easily combine modulus primes with this idea: If you pick a prime $p > m$, you can index bins as $h(x) \bmod p \bmod m$. Modulus p reduces the problem of regularity in keys, and if m is a power of two, you can grow and shrink tables easily. This also separates the concerns of computing a hash key from using hash keys to index into tables, as I wrote about the introduction chapter. You would have a two-step solution where you start with non-random numbers in $[N]$, map these using modul to $[p]$, and then continue as if your hash keys were originally uniformly distributed in $[p]$.

If your keys are randomly distributed, any m will do fine (and if both N and m are powers of two, you will get a uniform distribution in $[m]$). If you have such powers of two, $m = 2^k$, taking the remainder with respect to m is the same as masking out the lower k bits of the key. If the keys are random, the lower bits will also be random.

```
static inline unsigned int
hash_bin_index(struct hash_table *table, unsigned int key)
{
```

---

[1] This is less likely to happen to larger tables, but it is a concern for small tables.

```
unsigned int mask = table->size - 1;
unsigned int index = key & mask;
return index;
}
```

Subtracting one from the table size, $m = 2^k$, will give you the lower k bits, and masking with that provides you with the index.keez

Masking is a faster operation than modulo. In my experiments, I see about a factor of five in the speed difference. Compilers can optimize modulus to masking if they know that m is a power of two, but if m is a prime (and larger than two), this is of little help. How much of an issue this is depends on your application and choice of hash function. Micro-optimisations will matter very little if you have hash functions that are slow to compute.

If you are working with primes for m, there can be an advantage to working with Mersenne primes, i.e. those on the form $2^s - 1$. One such is $2^{61} - 1$, which can be a good choice for 32-bit words. Let $p = 2^s - 1$ and $x < p$. Write x on the form $a2^s + b$ ($b < 2^s$), that is, let $x \bmod 2^s = b$. Because $2^s \bmod p = 1$ we have $x \bmod p = a + b \bmod p$. Since we use integer division and $b < s^2$ we have $b/2^s = 0$ so we also have $x/2^s = a$. Because $x < 2^s - 1$, $x/2^s \bmod p = x/2^s$.

Now, let $y = (x \bmod 2^s) + (x/s^2)$. Again because $x < 2^s - 1$ we have $a < p$ so $a + b < 2p$. Therefore, either $y \leq p$ or $y \leq 2p$. If the former, that is $x \bmod p$; if the latter, then $x \bmod p = y - p$.

Because $x \bmod 2^x$ is the same as masking x by p and $x/2^s$ is the same as shifting x by s bits, we can compute modulo as this:

```
uint64_t mod_Mersenne(uint64_t x, uint8_t s)
{
    uint64_t p = (uint64_t)(1 << s) - 1;
    uint64_t y = (x & p) + (x >> s);
    return (y > p) ? y - p : y;
}
```

This avoids multiplications and modulo and only uses fast bit-operations. This will be much faster than modulo.

But enough theory. Let's get back to coding. We now have several ways to map a key to an index, so what remains for this section is to translate that into getting a bin. I prefer to write functions that give me pointers to bins. Then, I can inspect or update bins through those.

For the two kinds of bins we have considered, one where a bin is a struct and another where bins are unsigned int, such a function can look like this:

```
static inline struct bin *
hash_bin(struct hash_table *table, unsigned int key)
{
  return table->bins + hash_bin_index(table, key);
}
static inline unsigned int *
hash_bin(struct hash_table *table, unsigned int key)
{
  return table->bins + hash_bin_index(table, key);
}
```

They only differ in their return type.

Hash table operations

Once we have a function that maps keys to a bin, the three operations we need to implement are quite simple. When we insert an element, we get the bin and put the key there:

```
void
insert_key(struct hash_table *table, unsigned int key)
{
  struct bin *bin = hash_bin(table, key);
```

```
  if (bin->is_free) {
    bin->key = key;
    bin->is_free = false;
  } else {
    // There is already a key here, so we have a
    // collision. We cannot deal with this yet.
  }
}
```

when we have a bit to tell us if a bin is occupied and

```
void
insert_key(struct hash_table *table, unsigned int key)
{
  assert(key != RESERVED_KEY);
  unsigned int *bin = hash_bin(table, key);
  if (*bin == RESERVED_KEY) {
    *bin = key;
  } else {
    // There is already a key here, so we have a
    // collision. We cannot deal with this yet.
  }
}
```

when we have reserved a key for that purpose.

You will again notice that the two implementations are quite similar.

If the bin is already occupied, I don't do anything meaningful. We won't deal with it in this chapter, but it is the topic of the next chapter.

To check if a key is in the table, we follow the same pattern: we get hold of the bin and then check if the key is there. For the first version, we can do this:

```
bool
contains_key(struct hash_table *table, unsigned int key)
{
  struct bin *bin = hash_bin(table, key);
  // The bin contains the key if it isn't empty and the key
  // it contains is the one we are looking for.
  return !bin->is_free && (bin->key == key);
}
```

where we check if the bin is free before we check the key—to avoid accidentally mistaking random data for our key. For the alternate version were we use a special key value to indicate that nothing is stored in a bin, we do this:

```
bool
contains_key(struct hash_table *table, unsigned int key)
{
  return *hash_bin(table, key) == key;
}
```

We don't need to check if the bin is occupied or not; if it matches key and key is not allowed to be the reserved key, then comparing the value in the bin to the key suffices.

Finally, for deleting keys, the two versions can look like this:

```
void
delete_key(struct hash_table *table, unsigned int key)
{
  // Set the bin to free if the key matches, otherwise not
  // (it contains a different key)
```

```
  struct bin *bin = hash_bin(table, key);
  bin->is_free = (bin->key == key);
}
```

and

```
void
delete_key(struct hash_table *table, unsigned int key)
{
  unsigned int *bin = hash_bin(table, key);
  if (*bin == key) {
    *bin = RESERVED_KEY;
  }
}
```

Collision risk

We expect that hash key collisions are rare if they are the results of a well-designed hash function. Although collisions of hash keys are rare, however, it does not imply that we cannot get collisions in the indices. The range $[N]$ is usually vastly larger than the array indices in the $[m]$ range. Two different hash keys can easily end up in the same hash table bin, see Figure 2-1. Here, we have hash keys of size $N = 64$ and only $m = 8$ bins. The numbers next to the hash keys are written in octal, and we map keys to bins by extracting the lower eight bits of the key, which corresponds to the last digit in the octal representation. The keys 8 and 16, or 10_8 and 20_8 in octal, both maps to bin number 0, so they collide in the table.

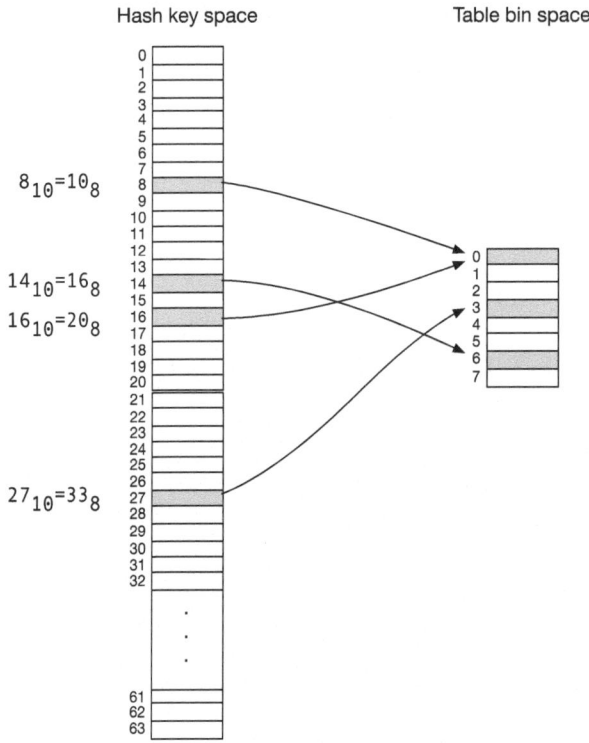

Figure 2-1. *Collisions of hash keys when binning them*

The figure is slightly misleading since the hash space is only a factor of eight larger than the hash table size. In any actual application, the keys range over a much wider interval than we could ever represent in a table. In the setup that we consider in this book, the range [N] maps over all possible unsigned integers, which is usually at least in the billions. This space is much larger than what you could reasonably use for an array—if you had to use your entire computer memory for a hash table, you would have no space for your computer program. Each value might map to a unique hash key, but we will likely see collisions when we have to map the hash keys down to a smaller range to store values in a table.

Assuming a uniform distribution of hash keys, we can do back-of-the-envelope calculations of collision probabilities. The chances of collisions are surprisingly high once the number of values approaches even a tiny fraction of the number of indices we can hit. To figure out the chances of collisions, we use the *birthday paradox*. In a room of n people, what is the probability that two or more have the same birthday? Ignoring leap years, we have 365 days in a year, so how many people do we need for the chance that at least two have the same birthday to be above one-half? This number, n, turns out to be very low. If we assume that each date is equally likely as a birthday, then with only 23 people we expect a 50% chance that at least two share a birthday.

We can phrase the problem of "at least two having the same birthday" a little differently. We can ask, "What is the probability that all n people have *different* birthdays?". The answer to the first problem will be one minus the answer to the second.

To answer the second problem, we can reason like this: out of the n people, the first birthday hits one out of 365 days without collisions. If we avoid collisions, the second person has to hit one of the remaining 364 days. The third one has to have his birthday on one of the 363 remaining days. Continuing this reasoning, the probability of no collisions on birthdays of n people is

$$\frac{365}{365} \times \frac{364}{365} \times \cdots \times \frac{365-n+1}{365}.$$

One minus this product is the risk of at least one collision when there are n people in the room. I have shown this probability as a function of the number of people in Figure 2-2. The curve crosses the point of 50% collision risk between 22 and 23.

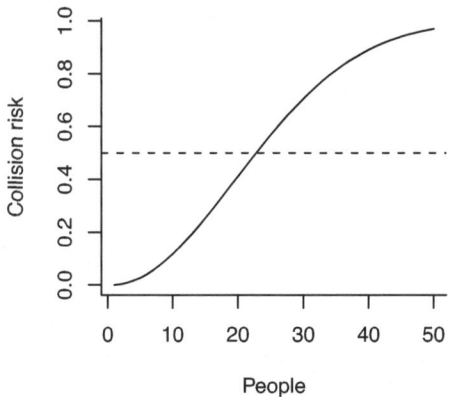

Figure 2-2. *The Birthday paradox*

The math carries over to an arbitrary number of "days", m, and tells us the risk of collision if we try to insert n elements into a hash table of size m. Provided that the keys are uniformly distributed in the range from 0 to $m - 1$, the probability that there is at least one collision is

$$p(n|m) = 1 - \frac{m!}{m^n (m-n)!}$$

See Figure 2-3 for a few examples of m and n.

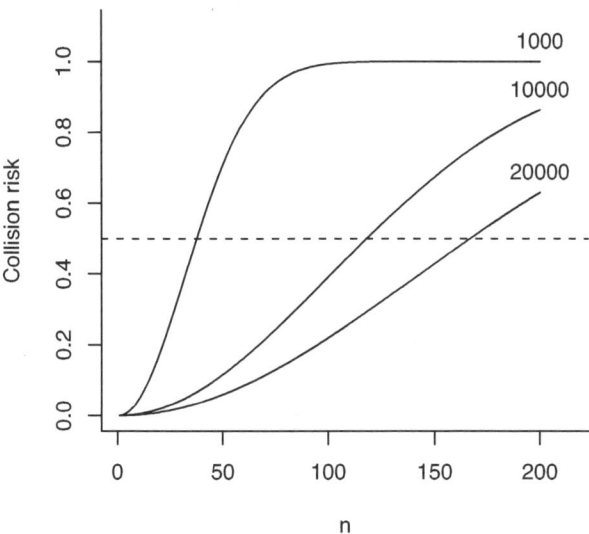

Figure 2-3. *Collision risks for different sizes of tables*

In practice, we are less interested in when the risk of collision reaches any particular probability than in how many items we can put into a table of size n before we get the *first* collision. Let K denote the random variable that represents the first time we get a collision when inserting elements into the table. The probability that the first collision is when we add item number k is

$$Pr(K=k\,|\,m)=\frac{m!}{m^{k}(m-k-1)!}\cdot\frac{k-1}{m}$$

where the first term is the probability that there were no collisions in the first $k-1$ insertions, and the second term is the probability that the k'th element hits one of the $k-1$ slots already occupied. The expected number of inserts we can do until we get the first collision can then be computed as

$$E[k\,|\,m]=\sum_{k=1}^{m+1}k{\cdot}Pr(K=k\,|\,m)$$

The sum starts at one where no collision is possible and ends at $m + 1$ where a collision is guaranteed. I have shown expected waiting time, together with sampled collision waiting times, in Figure 2-4.

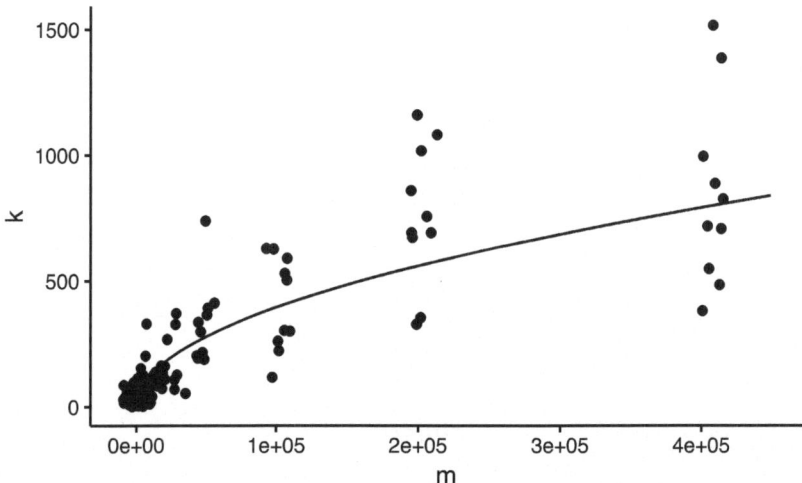

Figure 2-4. *Expected number of insertions before a collision*

It may not be immediately apparent from Figure 2-3 and Figure 2-4 what the relationship between m and k is for the risk of collision, but it should be evident that it is not linear. In Figure 2-3, increasing m by an order of magnitude when going from 1000 to 10,000 does not change the k where the risk is above 50% by an order of magnitude; the change is closer to a factor of three. Doubling m when going from 10,000 to 20,000 is far from doubling the k where we pass 50%. The expected number of elements we can insert into a table does not grow linearly with the size of the table is even more apparent from Figure 2-4, but how large should we have to make a table before we can expect to avoid collisions?

An approximation to the collision risk that is reasonably accurate for low probabilities is this:

$$p(k|m) \approx \frac{k^2}{2m}$$

I have shown this approximation as dashed lines in Figure 2-5.

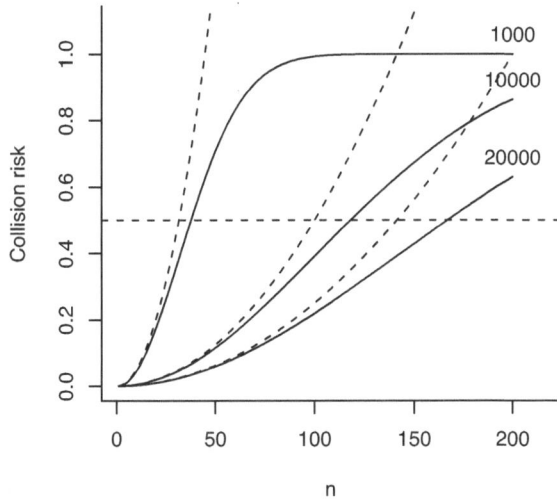

Figure 2-5. *Square approximation*

The approximation is unquestionably very poor at high probabilities—it tends to infinity, which is a bad approximation for a probability—but it is only slightly conservative at low probabilities. The good thing about this approximation is that it is easy to reason about it. We can rewrite it to:

$$m \approx \frac{k^2}{2p(k|m)}$$

The formula tells us that to keep the collision risk low, m has to be proportional to the square of k, with a coefficient that is inversely proportional to how low we want the risk.

This formula is potentially bad news. If we need to initialize the hash table before using it,[2] then we automatically have a quadratic time algorithm on our hands. That is a hefty price to pay for constant time access to the elements we put into the table. Since hash tables are used everywhere, this should tell you that, in practice, they do not rely on avoiding collisions entirely; they obviously have to deal with them—and most of this book is about how to do that.

Conclusion

As you have seen in this chapter, collisions are practically inevitable. Even if you were guaranteed that all hash keys were unique, they would still likely collide if you mapped them into a smaller number of bins. If you do not deal with collisions in a meaningful way, you have to use extremely large tables to reduce collision risk, incurring unacceptable overhead in memory usage and initialization time. However, as you shall see in the next chapter, there are techniques that allow you to deal with some level of collisions without sacrificing performance.

---

[2] It is technically possible to use the array in the table without initializing it, but it requires some trickery that incurs overhead.

CHAPTER 3

Collision Resolution, Load Factor, and Performance

Collisions are inevitable when using a hash table. At least if you want the table size—and thus the initialization time for the table—to be linear in the number of keys you put into it. Therefore, you need a way to deal with collisions so you can still insert keys if the bin you map it to is already occupied. There are two classical approaches to collision resolution: *chaining*—using linked lists to store colliding keys—and *open addressing*—where you find alternative empty slots to store values when keys collide.

You can download the complete code for this chapter from `https://github.com/mailund/JoyChapter3`.

Chaining

One of the most straightforward approaches to resolving collisions is to put colliding keys in a data structure that can hold them, and the most straightforward data structure is a linked list.

Linked Lists

The operations you need for storing elements in a list are these:

1. You should be able to add a new key to a list.

2. You should be able to test if a key is already there.

3. You should be able to remove a key from a list.

Also, you should be able to create and delete lists. For the links in a list, you can use this data structure:

```
struct link {
  unsigned int key;
  struct link *next;
};
```

This is as simple as it gets; any link contains a value and a pointer to the next link in the list. You use NULL for next to indicate that you are at the end of the list.

You can also define a list as a pointer to a link—and this is often how it is done—but that can complicate some operations. With a pointer to a link, you can only modify the link at hand and search further down the link, but you cannot change, for example, the previous link in the list. If you want to remove a link from a list, having a pointer to the link does you no good. You need a pointer to the previous link to update the previous link's next pointer to skip the link you want to delete. You need to keep track of the previous link to delete elements from a list. This is not the only reason that just having pointers to links is, at times, suboptimal. Ensuring that multiple references to the same list are kept in sync is difficult if you change the front link, for example, but access to the previous link is the key reason for this application.

If you want to represent lists so that you have access to a link *and* can modify the previous link, having a pointer to a pointer to a link turns out to be a good solution.

```
typedef struct link **LIST;
```

For many linked list operations, especially when inserting and deleting links, you need access to the previous link in a list so you can update its next pointer. Writing code that expects the previous link is a problem when you have to deal with the first link in a list, that by definition doesn't have a previous one. You could represent lists using some dummy link before the first real link, and this would alleviate the need for special cases, but in C, you can just as well get a pointer to a pointer to a link, which is what these lists are. If you have a pointer to a link, you also the address of that pointer, so you have a list for any link. The list can in most cases be thought of as "the previous link's next pointer," so in code that needs to modify that pointer, you have immediate access to it. However, the list representation is more general than that; it doesn't *have* to be the previous link's next pointer; it can be the address of any pointer to a link.

Because you are not directly pointing to links, you can have multiple references to the same list by having them all point to the pointer that, in turn, points to the beginning of the list (or NULL if the list is empty). When you traverse a list, you always point to the pointer pointing to the link you are currently addressing. When you start at the beginning of the list, you are pointing to the struct link * that the LIST is pointing at, and when you move along the next pointers, you keep a reference to the *address* of each next pointer. This way, when you need to delete something, you have the address of the next pointer you need to update so you can change it.

This might sound a bit complicated, but I hope it becomes clear when you get to the operations on the list.

To create a new list, you need a struct link pointer *and* a pointer to that pointer. This macro will give you such an object if you want to allocate the head of the list on the stack:

```
#define EMPTY_LIST &((struct link *){NULL})
```

You can use it like so:

```
  LIST static_list = EMPTY_LIST;
```

Or, if you want to allocate a list on the heap, you can use this:

```
LIST
new_owned_list()
{
    struct link **ptr = malloc(sizeof *ptr);
    *ptr = NULL;
    return ptr;
}
```

A newly allocated LIST is a pointer to a pointer, but the first thing you point to doesn't have to be a link. If it is NULL, you have an empty list. So, allocating a list on the heap involves allocating a pointer and setting it to NULL.

To free it again, you can use free().

```
void
free_owned_list(LIST list)
{
  free_list(list);
  free(list); // Freeing the heap allocated list
}
```

The free_list() function here is shared between stack and heap-allocated lists, and it runs through the links and frees them one by one:

```
static void
free_head(LIST list)
{
  struct link *next = (*list)->next;
  free(*list);
  *list = next;
}

void
free_list(LIST list)
{
  while (*list) {
    free_head(list);
  }
}
```

This might not be the usual way to write iterating through a list because you never directly move a pointer through the list. Instead, you have the head of the list in *list—the list variable contains a pointer to a pointer to a link, so *list is a pointer to the first link in the list. As long as *list isn't NULL, the list has links, so you get the second link in the list and put it in next, free the front, write the second list into list, and then you are ready for the following link.

The lists are not sorted, so if you insert a new key into a list, you can put it at the front:

```
struct link *
new_link(unsigned int key, struct link *next)
{
  struct link *link = malloc(sizeof *link);
  *link = (struct link){.key = key, .next = next};
  return link;
}
```

```
void
add_element(LIST list, unsigned int key)
{
  *list = new_link(key, *list);
}
```

To search the list and delete specific keys, you need to traverse the list until you find a given key. For this, you can write a help function that searches forward until the head of the list is the key you are searching for, or if it makes it through the list without finding the key, it will return NULL:

```
LIST
find_key(LIST list, unsigned int key)
{
  for (; *list; list = &(*list)->next) {
    if ((*list)->key == key)
      return list;
  }
  return NULL;
}
```

Checking if an element is in the list is now almost trivial to implement:

```
bool
contains_element(LIST list, unsigned int key)
{
  return find_key(list, key) != NULL;
}
```

Deleting the first link with a given key is almost as simple:

```
void
delete_element(LIST list, unsigned int key)
{
```

```
if ((list = find_key(list, key))) {
    free_head(list);
  }
}
```

This will only find and delete the first occurrence of key, but it is all you need. When you implement the hash table, you will ensure that you never insert the same key more than once.

Chained Hashing Collision Resolution

To use linked lists to resolve collisions, you replace the table of keys with an array of struct link **.

```
struct hash_table {
  struct link **bins;
  unsigned int size;
};
```

The type struct link ** is the type of LIST, but this doesn't mean that you use bins as a list. Instead, bins is an array of pointers to links, so any pointer *into* bins is a LIST.

The functions from the previous chapter for creating and deleting hash tables must be updated to initialize the bins as link pointers (initialized with NULL to get empty lists when you point into bins), and the lists must be freed when you free a table:

```
struct hash_table *
new_table(unsigned int size)
{
  struct hash_table *table = malloc(sizeof *table);
  table->bins = malloc(size * sizeof *table->bins);
  table->size = size;
```

```
  for (LIST bin = table->bins; bin < table->bins + table->size;
  bin++) {
    *bin = NULL;
  }
  return table;
}

void
free_table(struct hash_table *table)
{
  for (LIST bin = table->bins; bin < table->bins + table->size;
  bin++) {
    free_list(bin);
  }
  free(table->bins);
  free(table);
}
```

For the other three operations, you map the key to an index into the table as before and then call the appropriate operation on the linked list at that index:

```
LIST
get_key_bin(struct hash_table *table, unsigned int key)
{
  unsigned int mask = table->size - 1;
  unsigned int index = key & mask;
  return table->bins + index;
}

void
insert_key(struct hash_table *table, unsigned int key)
{
```

```
  LIST bin = get_key_bin(table, key);
  if (!contains_element(bin, key)) { // Avoid duplications
    add_element(bin, key);
  }
}

bool
contains_key(struct hash_table *table, unsigned int key)
{
  return contains_element(get_key_bin(table, key), key);
}

void
delete_key(struct hash_table *table, unsigned int key)
{
  LIST bin = get_key_bin(table, key);
  if (contains_element(bin, key)) {
    delete_element(bin, key);
  }
}
```

If you know your application will never have duplicated keys, you can leave out the check in the insert operation. It will likely matter little for the running time, since you aim to keep the lists short. Because you will keep the lists short, you don't have to worry about the linear search time in each list. If you have an application where you cannot resize your table to keep the number of collisions small, you can replace the linked lists with a more advanced data structure to speed up operations per bin, such as a search tree.

Open Addressing

The open addressing collision resolution does not use an extra data structure, but stores keys in the table as with direct addressing (the table implemented in the previous chapter). If there are collisions, however, and the desired index is already in use, the trick is to find another index to store the value. Somewhere that you can always find again, naturally.

Open addressing requires a strategy for searching for an available index when inserting an element. This search is called *probing*. To formalize this, you use a *probing strategy* $p(k, i)$, which gives you an index that depends on the hash-key, k, and an index, i, which goes from 0 to $m - 1$ where m denotes the size of the hash table. When you want to insert k into the table, you first attempt to add it at index $p(k, 0)$. If that slot is occupied, you instead try $p(k, 1)$, and if that slot is also occupied, you look at $p(k, 2)$, and so on. You want the strategy to probe the entire table eventually. That is, you want this sequence

$$p(k,0),p(k,1),p(k,2),\ldots,p(k,m-1)$$

to be a permutation of the numbers 0 to $m - 1$. That way, provided you haven't filled the entire table, you will eventually find an empty slot to put the key in.

Probing by iteratively checking if bins in the table are occupied creates a problem with deleting keys. If you remove keys by turning a table entry from occupied to empty, a later search will only get to this point before finding an empty bin and concluding that there are no more entries to probe. To solve this problem, you have to add another flag to the bin structure you used in direct hashing.

```
struct bin {
  unsigned int key;
  int in_probe : 1; // The bin is part of a sequence of used bins
```

```
  int is_empty : 1; // The bin does not contain a value (but
                    // might still be in a probe sequence)
};
```

The in_probe flag is true if a slot is part of a probe, so you should continue searching if you haven't found the key you are looking for yet. The is_empty flag is true if the slot is empty, so you can put a value there. When inserting a key, you can probe until you find a bin that is_empty. When you look up, you must continue until you find the key you are searching for or until you reach a bin that is not in_probe.

The structure for the hash table is the same as when there was no collision resolution.

```
struct hash_table {
  struct bin *bins;
  unsigned int size;
};
```

When you create a new table, you need to initialize each bin. Initially, no bin is in_probe, and all are is_free:

```
struct hash_table *
new_table(unsigned int size)
{
  struct hash_table *table = malloc(sizeof *table);
  table->size = size;
  table->bins = malloc(size * sizeof *table->bins);

  struct bin empty_bin = {.in_probe = false, .is_empty = true};
  for (unsigned int i = 0; i < size; i++) {
    table->bins[i] = empty_bin;
  }
```

```
  table->size = size;
  return table;
}
```

Freeing a table works the same as in the previous chapter. All the data is in the bins, so you only need to free that array and then the table structure:

```
void
free_table(struct hash_table *table)
{
  free(table->bins);
  free(table);
}
```

When inserting or looking for keys, you must use the probing strategy function to find the key or a free bin. In the next section, you see how to implement the probing strategy in this function:

```
static unsigned int
p(unsigned int key, unsigned int i, unsigned int m);
```

Its first argument is the hash function, the second is the index into the probe, and the last is the size of the hash table.

You can use the probe function to write two helper functions. One function finds the bin that contains a given key, if the key is in the table, or returns the first bin it finds that is not part of a probe. The second function finds the first empty bin.

```
struct bin *
find_key(struct hash_table *table, unsigned int key)
{
  for (unsigned int i = 0; i < table->size; i++) {
    struct bin *bin = table->bins + p(key, i, table->size);
    if (bin->key == key || !bin->in_probe)
      return bin;
  }
```

```
  // The table is full. We cannot handle that yet!
  assert(false);
}

struct bin *
find_empty(struct hash_table *table, unsigned int key)
{
  for (unsigned int i = 0; i < table->size; i++) {
    struct bin *bin = table->bins + p(key, i, table->size);
    if (bin->is_empty)
      return bin;
  }
  // The table is full. We cannot handle that yet!
  assert(false);
}
```

In the second, you only test if a bin is_empty and not whether it is in_probe, because you will have as an invariant that all bins not part of a probe are empty.

If you want to check if a key is in your table, you can use the find_key() function. If it returns a bin containing the key, which is not free, the key is in the table.

```
bool
contains_key(struct hash_table *table, unsigned int key)
{
  struct bin *bin = find_key(table, key);
  return bin->key == key && !bin->is_empty;
}
```

You need to check both if you have the key and if the bin is empty because it would be possible to accidentally reach the end of the probe and find a bin that, by pure chance, contained the key.

To delete a key, you can also use find_key(). If it returns a bin that contains the key, you set is_empty to true, and if it finds the end of the probe, it returns an empty probe where you can safely set is_empty to true without changing anything. So you can always set the result of find_key() to empty:

```
void
delete_key(struct hash_table *table, unsigned int key)
{
  find_key(table, key)->is_empty = true;
}
```

Finally, to insert a key, you need to find out if the key is already in the table—so you don't insert it twice—and if it isn't, you need to insert it at the first empty bin in the probe. You can use contains_key() for the first step and find_empty() for the second:

```
void
insert_key(struct hash_table *table, unsigned int key)
{
  if (!contains_key(table, key)) {
    *find_empty(table, key) =
        (struct bin){.in_probe = true, .is_empty = false,
        .key = key};
  }
}
```

Probing Strategies

Ideally, you want the probing strategy to map each key k to a random permutation of the indices $[m] = 0, 1, ..., m - 1$. In practice, this is easier said than done, and you can use simpler strategies. The most straightforward approach is *linear probing*. This strategy is far from a random permutation but is simple to implement. You search linearly from the index to get from the key to the end of the table, and then you wrap around and start from the beginning of the table.

$$p(k,i)=(k+i)\,mod\,m$$

I assume that you are using table sizes that are powers of two, which means that you can replace modulus with masking and implement probing like this:

```
static inline unsigned int
p(unsigned int key, unsigned int i, unsigned int m)
{
  return (key + i) & (m - 1);
}
```

There are two notable drawbacks to linear probing. First, if you have a collision, you not only collide on the first index but also on the entire probe sequence. This isn't that different from chaining, where you will also need to put colliding keys in the same list, but it is not ideal. You would expect that searching for an available bin would be faster if each key had a different probe sequence. Second, probe collisions will tend to cluster. If the linear probe sequence from one index overlaps the probe sequence starting at another index, the two probes will come into conflict. Keys that map to either index must probe to the end of the block of occupied bins.

Another strategy closer to the goal of getting a random permutation for each key is *double hashing*. The idea here is to use two different hash functions: one that maps the key to the initial index and one that determines the probe sequence. The form of the probe is this:

$$p(k,i)=h_1(k)+i\cdot h_2(k)\,mod\,m$$

For now, you can assume that the keys are already hash keys and thus uniformly distributed, so h_1 would always be the identity function. For h_2, you need some value that determines the probe sequence, and you have to make sure that it gives you a permutation of the numbers from 0 to $m - 1$. you get a probe that covers the entire range whenever m and $h_2(k)$ are mutual primes (i.e., their greatest common divisor is 1). Since you use hash table sizes that are powers of two, any hash function that gives you odd numbers will work, so a simple approach is to turn the key into an odd number by shifting the bits one position and setting the least significant bit to 1:

```
static inline unsigned int
p(unsigned int key, unsigned int i, unsigned int m)
{
    unsigned int h1 = key;
    unsigned int h2 = (key << 1) | 1;
    return (h1 + i*h2) & (m - 1);
}
```

As a fast but crude evaluation of the two strategies, you can sample the probe lengths in tables where you have inserted random keys. For the experiments in Figure 3-1, I built tables of size $m = 128$ and inserted n elements with $n = 32$, $n = 64$ and $n = 96$. I then sampled 1,000 random keys and measured the probe length for each. I also plotted the number of linked list cells examined in the chaining collision resolution strategy for comparison. As you can see, the probe lengths do not differ much when n is relatively small compared to m, but as n approaches m, the distribution of probe lengths for the linear probe shifts farther to the right than the double hashing. For both probing approaches, the open addressing strategy generally involves more probes than the chaining approach.[1]

---

[1] But don't write off open addressing because of this. The operations on the linked lists are usually more complicated and involve allocation of multiple memory blocks, which is less cache efficient. If you can keep the probe length small, open addressing can be more efficient than chaining.

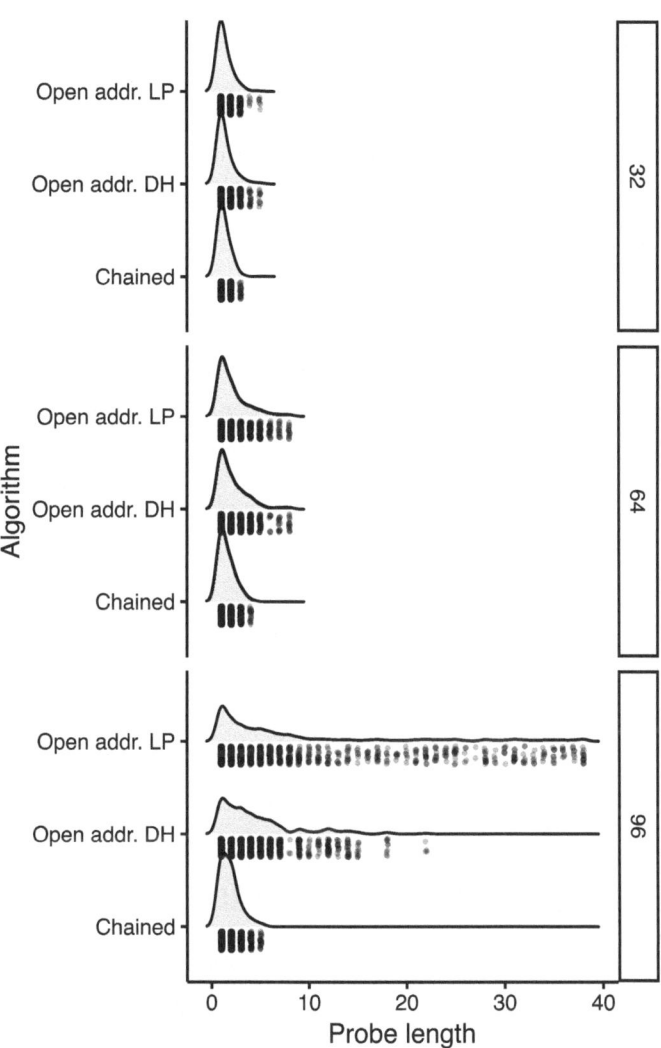

Figure 3-1. *Probe lengths for linear and double hashing probing*

Load and Performance

With conflict resolution strategies, you do not need to avoid collisions entirely, but collisions will still incur a performance penalty. If you can avoid collisions altogether, all operations take constant time, but as you start filling the table, the number of collisions will inevitably accumulate. The running time for each operation will degrade accordingly.

As a measure of how full a table is, you can define its *load factor*.

Definition: Given a hash table with m slots that store n elements, you define the *load factor* α for the table as $\alpha = n/m$.

This section considers the relationship between the running time and the load factor of a table using one of the two conflict resolution strategies you implemented. There are many theoretical results for worst-case and average-case performance of these strategies as functions of α; the proofs can be somewhat involved, so I do not show them here. Instead, I refer to algorithmic textbooks such as Sedgewick (1998)[2] Chapter 14 and Cormen et al. (2009),[3] Chapter 11, and the references in these.

I do, though, consider the consequences of the theoretical results and then explore performance through experiments.

Theoretical Runtime Performance

The two resolution strategies have different performance penalties as functions of the load factor. You should not be surprised by this, considering that chained hashing makes it impossible to fill a table to the point where you cannot insert more keys. You can always add new keys to one of the linked lists, regardless of how many keys you previously inserted

---

[2] Sedgewick, R. *Algorithms in C++, Parts 1–4: Fundamentals, Data Structure, Sorting, Searching, Third Edition.* (1998). Pearson Education

[3] Cormen, TH., Leiserson, CE., Rivest, RL. and Stein, C. *Introduction to Algorithms, Third Edition.* (2009). The MIT Press

into the table. With open addressing, you eventually run out of bins to put keys in. At this point, probing will either fail or enter infinite loops, depending on the implementation.

Chained Hashing

Chained hashing is the most straightforward strategy. The load factor for a chained hashing table is the average number of elements stored per linked list, assuming that keys are uniformly distributed. This follows from the observation that each bin is equally likely to be hit by a key if the keys are perfectly randomly distributed, and you map random keys in the key space into random bins in the table. From this observation follows:

Property (Theorem 11.1 Cormen et al): In a hash table in which chaining resolves collisions, both a successful and an unsuccessful search take time $\Theta(1 + \alpha)$, on average, under the assumption of uniform hashing.

If you are unfamiliar with Θ-notation, $\Theta(f(n))$ means that the running time of an algorithm tends to $c \cdot f(n)$ for some constant c as n tends to infinity. The Θ-notation is part of the terminology and notation known as "big-O" notation, where O-notation is most frequently used. If you say an algorithm runs in time $O(f(n))$, you mean that for some c, $c \cdot f(n)$ is an upper bound for the running time as n tends to infinity. Similarly, you use $\Omega(f(n))$ to indicate that $c \cdot f(n)$ is a lower bound for the running time of the algorithm as $n \to \infty$. Now, $\Theta(f(n))$ means that the algorithm has both $O(f(n))$ and $\Omega(f(n))$, that is, the running time of the algorithm will tend to $c \cdot f(n))$ for some constant c.

When using chaining conflict resolution, you are fundamentally relying on linked lists for your table. You use m of them, so you can shave off a factor of m in the running time compared to using a single linked list.

Open Addressing Hashing

With open addressing conflict resolution, you cannot reason as directly about conflicts as you can with chaining. Collisions can interfere; the probe starting at one table bin will overlap the probe beginning at another bin. There are theoretical results for the expected running time for table operations. The proofs are beyond this book, but these results show that the probe length depends on whether a search is successful (the key you search for is in the table) or not (the key you seek is not in the table).

Property (Property 14.3 Sedgewick): When collisions are resolved with linear probing, the average number of probes required to search in a hash table of size m that contains $n = \alpha m$ keys is about $\dfrac{1}{2}\left(1+\dfrac{1}{1-\alpha}\right)$

$$\text{and } \frac{1}{2}\left(1+\frac{1}{\left(1-\alpha\right)^2}\right)$$

for hits and misses, respectively.

Property (Property 14.4 Sedgewick): When collisions are resolved with double hashing, the average number of probes required to search in a hash table of size m that contains $n = \alpha m$ keys is about $\dfrac{1}{\alpha}log\left(\dfrac{1}{1-\alpha}\right)$

$$\text{and } \frac{1}{1-\alpha}$$

for hits and misses, respectively.

I plotted these theoretical results in Figure 3-2.

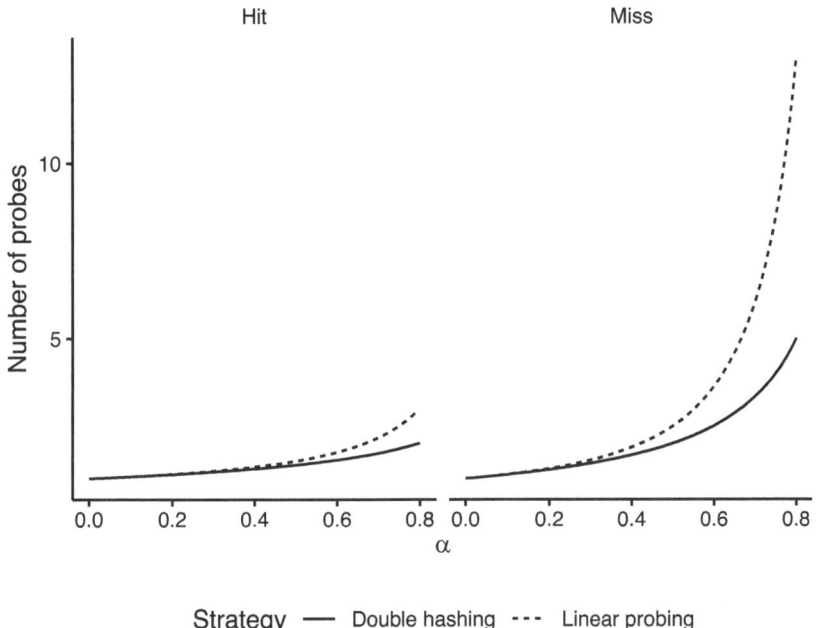

Figure 3-2. *Theoretical probe length as a function of load*

While the running time for chained collision resolution tends to be linear as the load factor grows, even when $\alpha > 1$, the running time for open addressing tends to infinity as α approaches 1. This is true only if you ignore the actual size of the hash table and do not discover infinite loops. Suppose the table has size m, and you avoid infinite loops when probing for an empty slot. In that case, you should never have probes longer than m, so in practice, the running time for open address conflict resolution tends toward m as the load factor tends toward 1. Of course, as α tends to 1, the chained collision resolution doesn't tend toward linear running time in a practical sense either. As $\alpha \to 1$, the probe length tends toward 1 as well, since, with n keys in a table of size m, you expect the average linked list to have length $\alpha = n/m$, so you expect, on average, to have probe length 1. As the load factor tends toward 1, the chained hashing strategy degrades more gracefully than the open addressing strategy. With the open addressing strategy, the double hashing strategy will give you shorter probes than linear probing.

Using the implementations from the previous section, you can validate the theoretical results experimentally. I constructed tables of size $m = 1024$ and varied n from 32 to 900 (with an α from 0.03125 to 16.0) and counted how many probes each method needed when looking up a random key (which, since the space of possible keys is much larger than n, is most likely a miss). I plotted the results in Figures 3-3 and 3-4, with the full range of load factors shown in Figure 3-3 and the load factors smaller than 1/2 shown in Figure 3-4 (in the full range, the results for small load factors are drowned out by the long probes at high load factors). The lines are loess-fitted smoothings of the data, roughly showing the mean values along the load axis. The experimental results show the same pattern as you would expect from the theoretical results. The chaining approach has the probe length grow linearly as a function of the load factor. In contrast, the open addressing probe length grows super-linearly while approaching 1, with the linear probe strategy growing faster than the double hashing strategy.

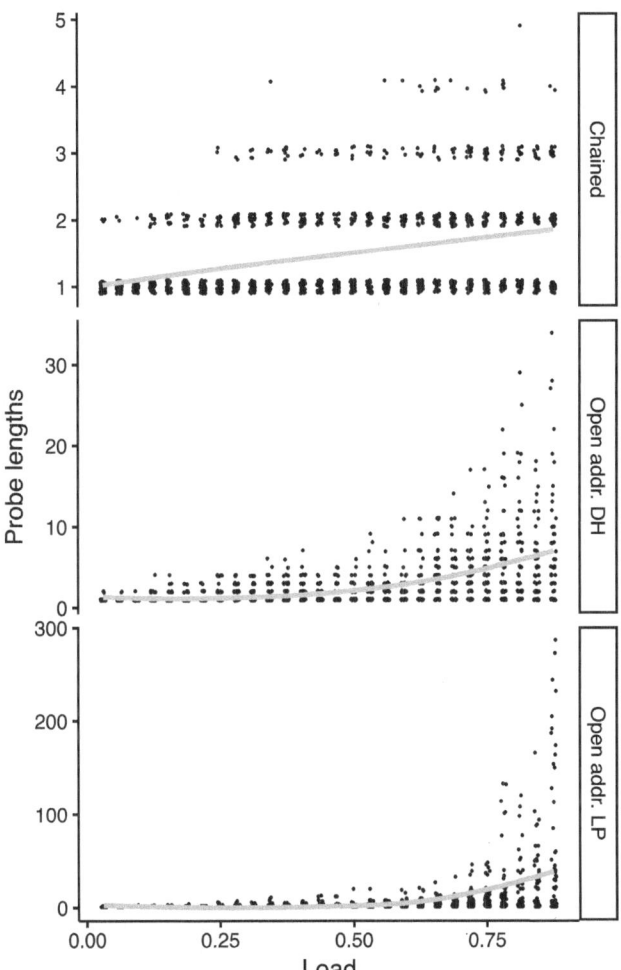

Figure 3-3. *Number of probes for different load factors*

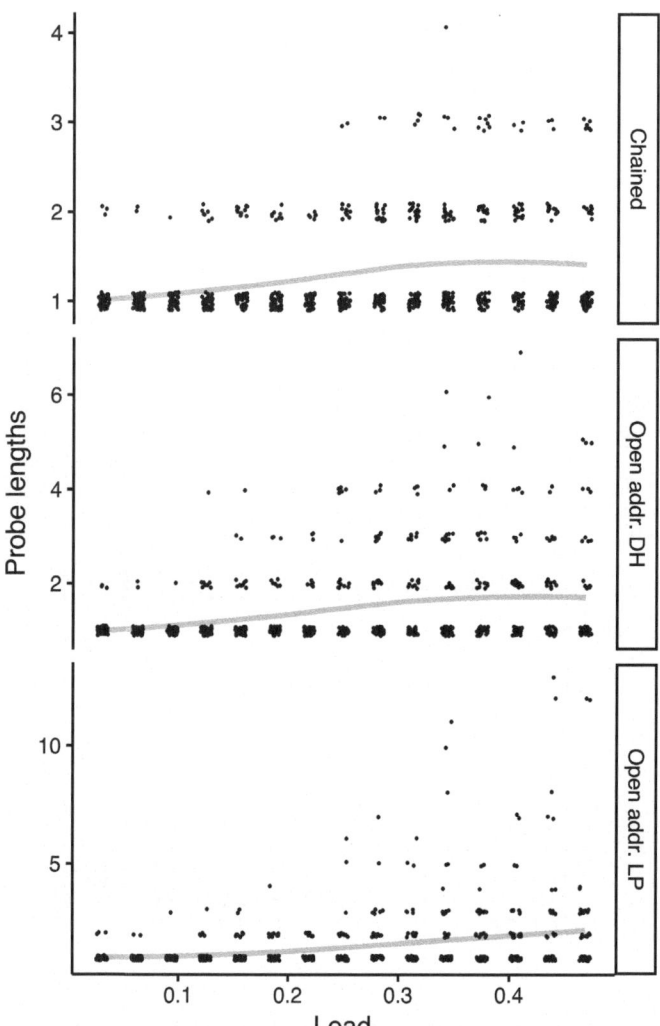

Figure 3-4. *Number of probes for different small load factors*

In Figure 3-5, the dots are the mean probe lengths for each load factor, and the dashed lines are the theoretical expectations.

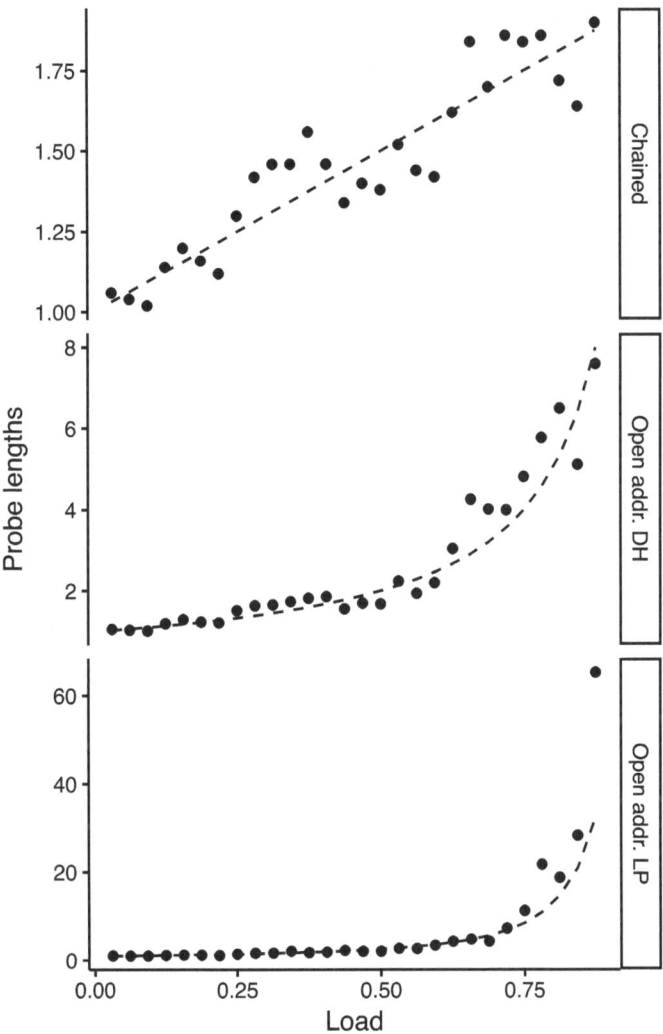

Figure 3-5. *Mean probe lengths vs. theoretical probe lengths*

Probe lengths aren't everything, however. The cost involved with each probe matters as well. For linked lists, there is some overhead involved, although it is relatively minor, and this overhead might make open addressing more appealing as long as you keep $\alpha \ll 1$. Also, while the double-hashing strategy gives you shorter probes, this comes at the cost of evaluating two hash functions instead of one. On top of this, there is cache efficiency to consider. With chained hashing, you need to allocate list links, and all links in any given list are not necessarily found close together in memory. With double hashing, you jump around in the table of bins, and this is not cache-efficient. You search bins close together in memory with linear probing, which might compensate for the longer probe sequences. The optimal strategy might very well depend on your application and can only be examined by considering actual implementations.

Experiments

To evaluate the time usage for the three different collision resolution methods, I once again constructed tables of size 1024 (a power of two since you map keys to bins by masking) and then inserted n elements, varying n from 32 to 900 (with an α from 0.03125 to 16.0). After populating the tables, I performed 1,000 lookups with random keys (which means that you are vastly more likely to have misses in the search than hits, thus providing conservative runtime results). Figure 3-6 shows the results for the entire range of load factors. The x-axis is on a log scale, which is why the chained collision resolution strategy does not appear as a line.

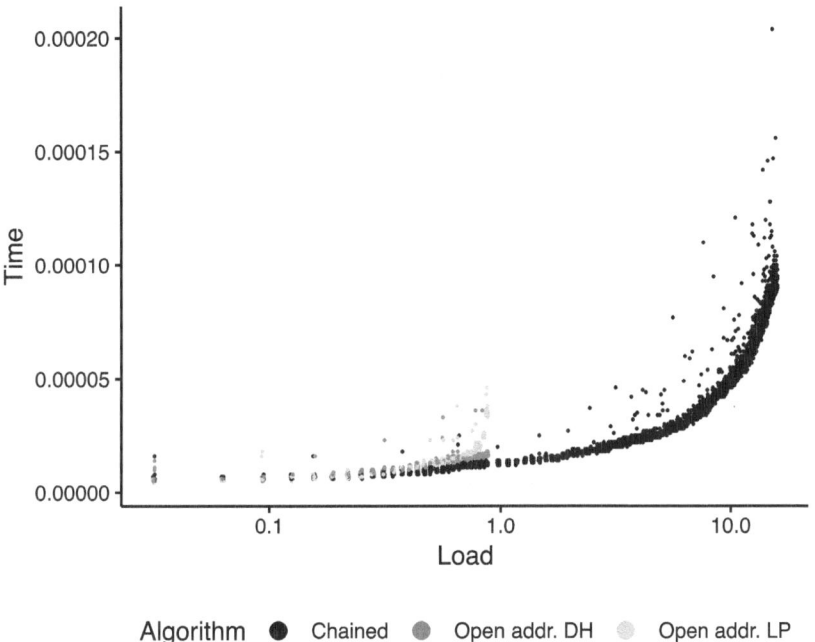

Algorithm ● Chained ● Open addr. DH ○ Open addr. LP

Figure 3-6. *Lookup time usage as a function of load*

Overall, you see the degradation in performance in open addressing collision resolution as the load factor approaches 1, while the chained collision resolution degrades more gracefully. Also note that the linear probing strategy gets slower than the double hashing strategy as the load factor approaches 1.

You might expect shorter probes with double hashing, but as observed in the previous section, this comes at the cost of more expensive probe operations. Consider low load factors; see Figures 3-7 and 3-8, where the latter displays the same information as the former but is less cluttered since it only shows the mean time for each load factor instead of each replication. These plots focus on small load factors. You can see that at small load factors, $\alpha < 0.2$, the linear probe, with its small computational overhead, is the fastest. The double hashing implementation overtakes linear probing around $\alpha = 0.45$, but long before that, at $\alpha = 0.2$, the linked list chaining is fastest (and remains so as α grows).

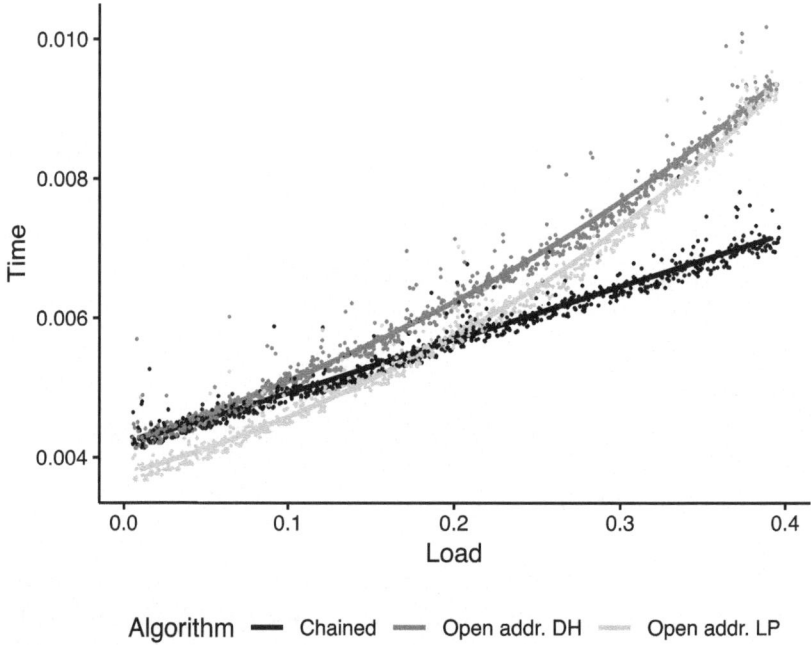

Figure 3-7. *Lookup time usage as a function of load*

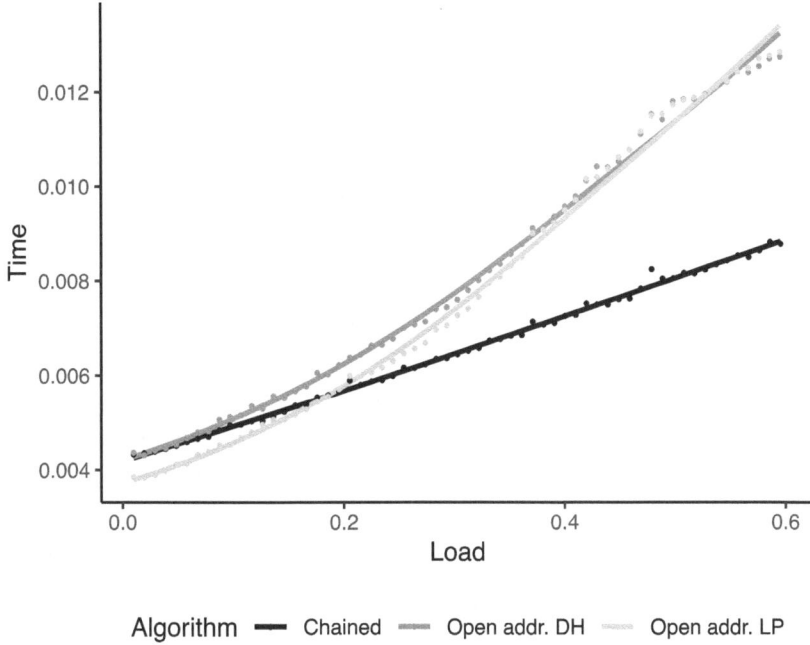

Figure 3-8. *Mean lookup time usage as a function of load*

The exact ranges of load factors at which the different conflict resolution methods dominate in runtime will depend on the implementations, runtime systems, and the hardware you run the experiments on. In general, however, at small load factors, linear probing, with the lowest overhead, will be best. As α approaches 1, the chaining approach will be best (and it will, naturally, be the only approach that works for $\alpha \geq 1$).

However, it is only partially fair to say that chained hashing is out-competing the open addressing tables just from these experiments. You should also consider cache efficiency. In these experiments, the tables are all relatively small, so you do not see a cache effect, but for larger tables, you will. Dynamically allocated links for the lists in chained hashing are non-optimal for cache usage unless you implement your lists to explicitly avoid it. Allocating links to minimize cache misses is far from trivial. You will need to allocate memory pools for the links, and you will want to have separate pools for each bin, so searching through the keys in any given bin will involve searching in a list where the links are located close to each other in memory. If you jump around too much in memory as you scan through a list, you will see many cache misses, and the performance will degrade accordingly.

Because the bins in open addressing tables are allocated in contiguous memory locations, caching performance is likely better. If all your bins fit into a cache line, open addressing is very efficient. If they do not, linear probing will have fewer cache misses. As you scan linearly through the bins, your probes access nearby memory locations, which is optimal for cache efficiency. With double hashing, you will jump around in memory; you would, therefore, expect more cache misses. Although the probe lengths might be longer for linear hashing, the improved cache performance can easily compensate for this. In Figure 3-9, I plotted the runtime for larger table sizes (all with load 0.5). Here, you can see that open addressing outperforms chained hashing once the tables are large enough where cache efficiency is an issue, even in the load range where chained hashing outperforms open addressing for smaller tables.

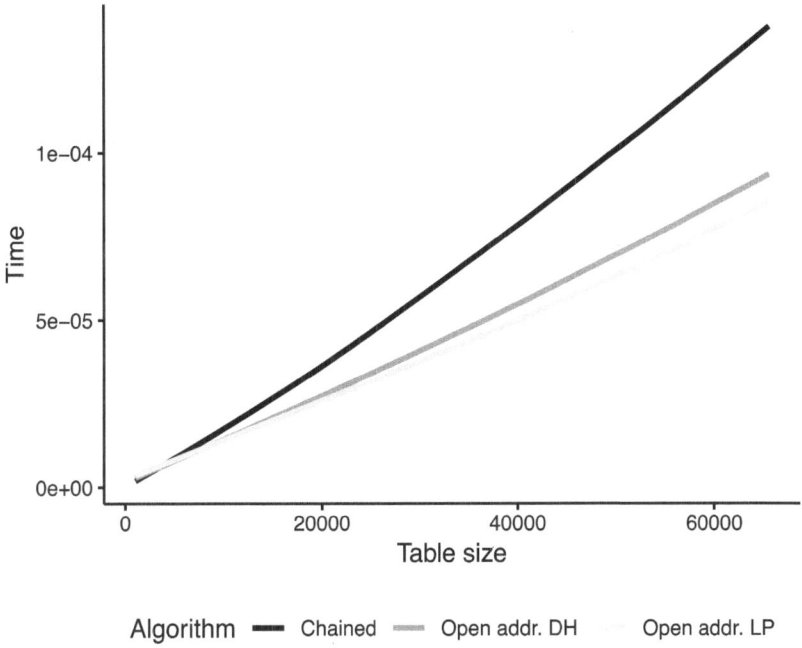

Figure 3-9. *Table size vs time*

Many considerations will affect the performance of your hash tables, and there are many tradeoffs. There isn't one best solution, as it depends on your application. If the performance of a hash table is critical to your application, it might be worthwhile to experiment with different solutions and engineer your table to be optimal for the specific usage you will subject it to.

Conclusion

You have now seen techniques for alleviating the problem of collisions, at least when you do not have too many of them. With the chained hashing strategy, you can in principle deal with any number of collisions, but the performance will degrade linearly with the number of elements you put in a table. With open addressing hashing, the performance degrades dramatically after a point. With this strategy, you can never deal with more elements than you have bins. If you can deal with some collisions, but not too many, you need a way to scale the size of your tables with the number of elements they contain. That is the topic of the next chapter.

CHAPTER 4

Resizing

If you know how performance degrades as the load factor of a hash table increases, you can use this information to pick a table size where the expected performance matches your needs—presuming that you know how many keys the table will need to store. If you do not know the number of elements you need to keep, n, you cannot choose a table size, m, which ensures that $\alpha = n/m$ is below a desired upper bound. In most applications, you do *not* know n before you run the program. Therefore, you must adjust m as n increases by resizing the table.

You can download the code from this chapter from `https://github.com/mailund/JoyChapter4`.

Whenever you resize a hash table from size m_{old} to m_{new}, you need to create a new array of length m_{new}. After that, you need to copy all the elements from the old table's bins into the new table's bins (where the keys are expected to be more spread out if the new array is larger than the old array). Allocating the new array and initializing its bins takes time $O(m_{new})$ and moving elements from the old array to the new also takes time $O(n) = O(\alpha \cdot m_{old} + m_{old})$. If the load factor is bounded by some constant, resizing a table takes time proportional to the new table size. This runtime cost tells you that you cannot be too aggressive with resizing. If you aim to keep the load factor small to guarantee constant time lookups, you should not expect to pay for this through linear time updates.

Amortizing Resizing Costs

Resizing a table takes time $O(m_{new})$ (as long as $\alpha \le 1$), so you cannot guarantee an expected constant running time for all operations if insertion or deletion can trigger resizing. Most operations might take constant time—or be expected to be constant time, as the actual time depends on the length of linked lists or the length of open addressing probes. If an operation requires that you resize the table, however, that operation will not run in constant time. Instead of ensuring constant time operations, you can achieve something almost as good; that you can always perform n operations in expected time $O(n)$.

Such a guarantee is known as an *amortized* running time.[1] The way you amortize the resizing of hash tables is similar to how you implement a stack using a "growable array." This structure is simpler than a hash table, so you first see the trick there, and then take it to the hash table afterwards.

The abstract interface of a stack allows you to check if it is empty, push elements on it, and pop elements from it. The interface could look like this:

```
struct stack *new_stack(int initial_size);
void free_stack(struct stack *stack);

bool is_empty(struct stack *stack);
void push(struct stack *stack, int value);
int pop(struct stack *stack);
```

---

[1] Strictly speaking, *amortized* means that you write off expensive operations over time, and this suggests that cheaper ones follow costly operations. Doing this would not give you the runtime guarantee you are after, however. If you stop an algorithm right after an expensive operation and do not follow it with a series of cheap operations, you will be in trouble; you will not be meeting the runtime guaranteed. What you do with amortized running time is save up some "computation" when doing cheap operations such that you can guarantee that you have enough computation in your "bank account" when you need to pay for an expensive operation.

If you implement a stack using an array, the stack structure will hold this array, and you can keep track of how many elements are in the stack to access the top of the stack.

```
struct stack {
  int *array;
  unsigned int used;
};
```

If used moves past the size of the array, however, you need to resize it. For this, you need a growable array.

A *growable array* is a data structure that you can append to in amortized constant time as well as update and access elements in worst-case constant time. Updating and accessing elements work just as for arrays; you keep values in contiguous memory and can access them through a pointer and an index. Because you use contiguous memory, appending might have to add an element that doesn't fit in the space you have allocated. When this happens, you need to resize the underlying allocated array.

To keep track of both the size of the array and the number of used entries, you can update the stack with an additional counter:

```
struct stack {
  int *array;
  unsigned int size;
  unsigned int used;
};
```

Creating and deleting a stack is straightforward, and similar to what you have done with hash tables so far:

```
struct stack *
new_stack()
{
```

```
  struct stack *stack = malloc(sizeof *stack);
  *stack = (struct stack){.size = 1,
                          .used = 0,
                          .array = malloc(sizeof *stack->
                          array)};
  return stack;
}

void
free_stack(struct stack *stack)
{
  free(stack->array);
  free(stack);
}
```

Checking if a stack is empty is even simpler:

```
bool
is_empty(struct stack *stack)
{
  return stack->used == 0;
}
```

For pushing and popping, you mostly do what you would expect—add an element at index used or return the element there—but you might also trigger a resize operation if you have grown to the point where there is no additional space, or if you have shrunk the stack so that you can use less memory.

```
void
push(struct stack *stack, int value)
{
  if (stack->used == stack->size)
    resize(stack, 2 * stack->size);
```

```
  stack->array[stack->used++] = value;
}

int
pop(struct stack *stack)
{
  int top = stack->array[--(stack->used)];
  if (stack->used < stack->size / 4)
    resize(stack, stack->size / 2);
  return top;
}
```

The choice of when to shrink the array is described soon.

Resizing the array is a simple call to `realloc()`:

```
static void
resize(struct stack *stack, unsigned int new_size)
{
  stack->array = realloc(stack->array, new_size * sizeof
  *stack->array);
  stack->size = new_size;
}
```

When an append triggers a resize, you double the allocated memory. You use `realloc()` to automatically free the old array and automatically copy the old elements into the new when necessary. When you resize hash tables later, you need to move elements because you also need to map the keys to new bins. You cannot use `realloc()` so easily, but you can implement resizing by explicitly moving elements.

Growing the size by a constant factor—two when you double the size—is crucial for getting amortized constant time. If you instead chose to increase the length just enough to store the next element, resizing becomes prohibitively expensive. Each time you resize the array, you need to allocate new memory and move all the existing values to the new array. This takes time proportional to the length of the array. If you started with an array of size 1 and pushed n elements onto the array, you would use time $1 + 2 + \cdots + n - 1 + n = n(n - 1)/2 = O(n^2)$.

If you double the array size each time you grow, it lets you append m elements in time $O(m)$. In general, increasing the array size by any fixed factor $\beta > 1$ will do this; I return to this later in this chapter. I first consider doubling the size. To see that m appends can be done in time $O(m)$, consider the appends between two successive resizing calls. Let the size of the append just after the first size increase be m and the size after the second be $2m$. When you increased the size to m, you did this from $m/2$ and a full array, so the state just after the increase has a half-full array (that is, the array has length m and contains $m/2$ elements). You need to append an additional m/2 elements to get to the next resizing. The first $m/2 - 1$ of these operations takes constant time. The last takes constant time for appending the last element, then uses time $2m$ for allocating a new array, and finally uses time m for copying all the items to the new array. So in total, the $m/2$ operators take time $m/2 - 1 + 1 + 4m/2 + 2m/2 = 7m/2$, which is in $O(m)$.

There is another way to put it: you can make each append cost seven "computations." Of these seven, one is used on the append, and six are put in the bank. After the $m/2 - 1$ appends, the bank contains $6(m/2 - 1)$ computations. If you include the seven from the last append, making this operation pay one "computation" immediately and put the remaining six in the bank as the other operations did, you have $6m/2$ left in the bank before you resize. That number of banked operations is what you need to allocate a new array of size $2m$ ($4m/2$) and copy m elements ($2m/2$).

Resizing is illustrated in Figure 4-1. Here, the first (dark gray) block represents the elements that you copied from the previous $m/2$-sized array into the size m array. The next block (light gray) is the $m/2$ long block into which you can insert elements. When you have inserted all these, you must allocate the $2m$ sized array and move both dark and light gray elements, m elements in total, to the new array.

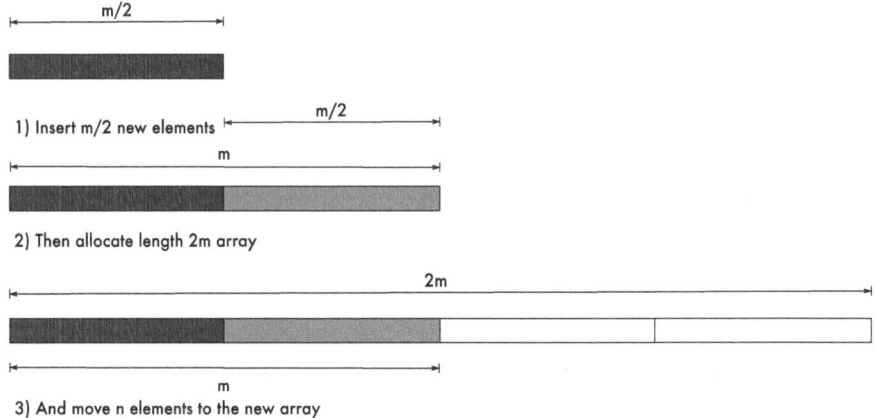

Figure 4-1. *Illustration of the steps to go from one enlargement of the array to another*

Figure 4-2 shows the running time when growing an array each time you fill it up. The graph shows the number of operations spent on actually inserting elements, allocating memory for them, and moving them from the old array to the new, and then the cost of all the operations combined in the total running time. The linear upper bound $7m$, which you just derived, is shown as a dashed line.

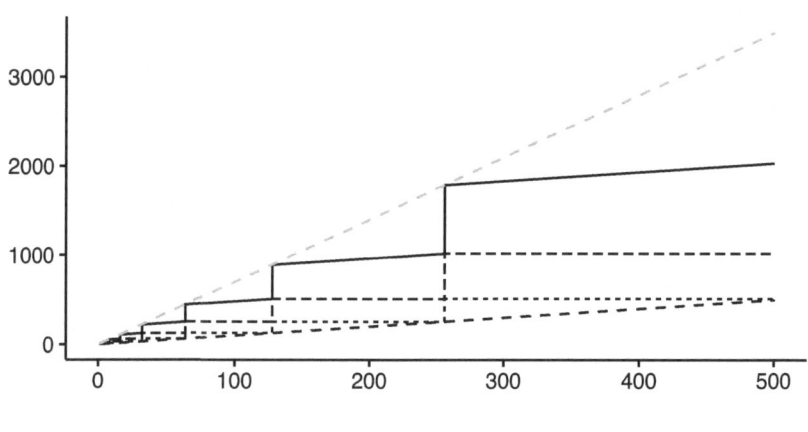

Figure 4-2. *Illustration of the running time when growing an array by doubling it each time it gets filled*

This analysis assumes that you move from one resize operation to the next as early as you can, by appending $m/2$ times in a row. If you include the other operations, and let them put elements in the bank, you only end up with a larger account before you need to resize.

Growing the array suffices if you only want to ensure that you can store all the elements you ever need to hold, but it can be a waste of memory if you only hold this maximum number of items early in a program and hold much fewer items after that. As an example of this, you can introduce a "pop" operation that removes the last element and shrinks the array to reduce memory usage. For shrinking, you need to insert coins in the bank when popping to pay for resizing and get amortized running time.

You can halve the length of the array when you have popped the array to a sufficiently small size and choose the quarter of the allocated size for "sufficiently low."

With this choice, you can pop m times in time $O(m)$. Consider the pops between two resize operations. Let the first resizing be one that leaves the length of the array at m and the second one that reduces the size to $m/2$. Between these two resize operations, you must have appended $m/4$ elements. The resize to m would have left the table containing $m/2$ elements (regardless of whether the resize operation grew or shrunk the array), and you do not shrink the array to length $m/2$ before it only contains $m/4$ elements.

If you move directly from the m'th resize event to the $m/2$ resizing, you must have performed $m/4$ pops where the first $m/4 - 1$ involves $m/4 - 1$ constant time pops and the last involves one operation for popping and then $m/2$ (for allocating the new array) plus $m/4$ (for copying elements), so in total $m/4 - 1 + 1 + 2m/4 + m/4 = m$. Using the banking analogy, you can charge each pop four, one for the pop and three for the bank. If you do this, you have $3m/4$ in the bank when you need to resize and copy. Resizing costs $2m/4$ and copying costs $m/4$.

Now consider the hash tables. The resizing strategy for those is similar to the array. The thresholds for when you grow or shrink a table can be the same for chained hashing as for the stack: you grow when you have "filled" the table by having a load of $\alpha = 1$, and you shrink it to half that size when the load is a quarter, $\alpha 1/4$.

For open addressing hashing, you cannot allow the hash table to fill up before you grow it. The performance degrades dramatically as the load factor approaches 1. You need to resize the tables before α gets too close to 1. Any fixed load factor will do, but as an initial choice, you grow tables when $\alpha = 1/2$, which gives you a new load factor of $1/4$, and shrink them when $\alpha = 1/8$, which also gives you a load factor of $1/4$. This will keep the load factor for any resizable tables between $1/8$ and $1/2$, and those load factors should provide excellent performance, according to the calculations in the previous chapter.

The runtime analysis for resizing works analogous to the analysis for arrays. You have to bank a bit more for each cheap operation, but otherwise, the analysis is the same. Between growing a table from size m to size $2m$, you need to increase the number of keys stored in the table from $m/4$ to $m/2$ ($m/4$ constant time operations) and then allocate the new table ($2m$) and copy the elements ($m/2$), for a total of $m/4 + 8m/4 + 2m/4 = 11m/4$. So, you can charge each insertion 11. The $m/4$ insertions cost $m/4$ directly and leave $10m/4$ in the bank, while allocating the new array costs $2m$, which leaves $m/2$ in the bank. You can use this to pay for the $m/2$ elements you need to copy.

For deletion, consider the operations between resizing to m and shrinking to $m/2$. Here, you need to remove $m/8$ elements (after resizing to size m, the table contains $m/4$ elements and you shrink when you reach $m/8$). The resizing costs $m/2$ and the copying costs $m/8$, so during the $m/8$ delete operations, you need to save up $5m/8$. If you charge each delete $6m/8$, you can pay for the deletion and save many computations for the resizing.

A final modification to the hash tables compared to the stack is that you will give them a minimum size. This size *could* be one, as the stack, but it does not make much sense to resize the tables when they are tiny. So, you give them a minimal size, for example

```
#define MIN_SIZE 8
```

New tables will have at least this many bins, and you will never shrink them below this size. This doesn't change the amortization calculations, but you avoid allocating and reallocating small blocks of memory.

Resizing Chained Hash Tables

The overall pattern for resizing hash tables is the same for the different strategies. You check a used variable against the size variable after each insert or deletion. If you trigger a resize, you allocate a new array of bins, initialize it, and copy all elements from the old array to the new one. The details differ slightly between chained hashing and open addressing, however, so let's consider the two strategies separately. Let's start with chained hashing.

First, you need to make sure you keep track of the size and the number of keys stored in the table. For this, you need the two variables: `size` and `used`.

```
struct hash_table {
  struct link **bins;
  unsigned int size;
  unsigned int used;
};
```

When you create a table, you initialize it with at least `MIN_SIZE` bins, and you store that in its `size`, but otherwise, there is not much change compared to the previous chapter.

```
static void init_bins(struct hash_table *table)
{
  for (LIST bin = table->bins; bin < table->bins + table->size;
  bin++) {
    *bin = NULL;
  }
}

struct hash_table *
new_table()
{
  struct hash_table *table = malloc(sizeof *table);
  struct link **bins = malloc(MIN_SIZE * sizeof *bins);
  *table = (struct hash_table){.bins = bins, .size = MIN_SIZE,
  .used = 0};
  init_bins(table);
  return table;
}
```

You might trigger a resize every time you insert or delete a key. You only want to risk this when you *actually* insert or delete a key, so you first check if the key in question is in the table, and if it is, you will trigger the resize operation after the insertion or deletion. With the stack, you resized before inserting, but it doesn't really matter with a chained hash table since you cannot run out of bins, and it is easier to insert or delete first since you have the bin for the key as part of the lookup operation, and this bin would change in a resize.

So, insertion and deletion can be implemented like this:

```
void
insert_key(struct hash_table *table, unsigned int key)
{
  LIST bin = get_key_bin(table, key);
  if (!contains_element(bin, key)) {
    add_element(bin, key);
    table->used++;
    if (table->size == table->used) {
      resize(table, 2 * table->size);
    }
  }
}

void
delete_key(struct hash_table *table, unsigned int key)
{
  LIST bin = get_key_bin(table, key);
  if (contains_element(bin, key)) {
    delete_element(bin, key);
    table->used--;
    if (table->size > MIN_SIZE && table->used
    < table->size / 4) {
```

```
    resize(table, table->size / 2);
    }
  }
}
```

When resizing, you need to allocate a new array for the bins and then copy all the links from the old bins to the new ones. You can split this into two functions. The first function allocates the new bins and calls the other to move the links:

```
static void
resize(struct hash_table *table, unsigned int new_size)
{
  // Remember these so we can copy and free the old bins
  struct link **old_bins = table->bins, **old_from = old_bins,
               **old_to = old_from + table->size;

  // Set up the new table
  table->bins = malloc(new_size * sizeof *table->bins);
  table->size = new_size;
  init_bins(table);

  // Copy links from the old bins to the new ones
  copy_links(table, old_from, old_to);

  // Free the old bins memory
  free(old_bins);
}
```

Finally, you can copy the links from the old array to the new one by moving each link:

```
static void
copy_links(struct hash_table *table, LIST from, LIST to)
{
```

```
for (; from < to; from++) {
  while (*from) {
    struct link *link = *from;
    // Remove the first link from old bin by replacing
    // it by its next.
    *from = link->next;
    // Connect the link to the new bin.
    LIST new_bin = get_key_bin(table, link->key);
    link->next = *new_bin;
    *new_bin = link;
  }
 }
}
```

Resizing Open Addressing Hash Tables

For open addressing, there is a tiny complication: deleted elements still take up space in the table. When you insert elements, you increase the load, but when you delete them, you only "kinda" decrease it. When you delete an element, you mark its bin as "free," but it will still be part of the probes. So, if you are searching for a free bin, the load has indeed decreased, but if you are searching for a key, it hasn't. The load factor indicates how many keys a table holds, but deleted elements slow down contains_key and, consequently, both insertion and deletion operations, as much as keys that are still in the table.

To know when to grow the table to ensure good performance, the used counter has to count both the number of keys in the table and the number of deleted elements. This means that you cannot decrease used when you delete elements, which is a problem if you want to shrink tables as well as grow them.

You can get around this issue by using two counters instead of one. The first, used, counts how many bins are part of the probes—either because a bin contains a key or because it holds a key that was previously deleted. The second, active, only counts the number of bins that hold an actual key. The updated hash_table structure will look like this:

```
struct hash_table {
  struct bin *bins;
  unsigned int size;
  unsigned int used;
  unsigned int active;
};
```

You can create and free tables like this:

```
struct hash_table *
new_table()
{
  struct hash_table *table = malloc(sizeof *table);
  init_table(table, MIN_SIZE, NULL, NULL);
  return table;
}

void
delete_table(struct hash_table *table)
{
  free(table->bins);
  free(table);
}
```

You will learn more about the init_table() function later, but it will set up the bookkeeping in the hash table and allocate the bins to the size given as its second argument. The third and fourth arguments are used when you resize a table.

Use the same two helper functions as before:

```
struct bin *
find_key(struct hash_table *table, unsigned int key)
{
  for (unsigned int i = 0; i < table->size; i++) {
    struct bin *bin = table->bins + p(key, i, table->size);
    if (bin->key == key || !bin->in_probe)
      return bin;
  }
  // The table is full. This should not happen!
  assert(false);
}

struct bin *
find_empty(struct hash_table *table, unsigned int key)
{
  for (unsigned int i = 0; i < table->size; i++) {
    struct bin *bin = table->bins + p(key, i, table->size);
    if (bin->is_empty)
      return bin;
  }
  // The table is full. This should not happen!
  assert(false);
}
```

They don't change just because you keep track of the table size, but this time you should never get to a full table, so the assert()s are only for show.

Looking up a key is also the same as in the previous chapter:

```
bool
contains_key(struct hash_table *table, unsigned int key)
{
```

```
  struct bin *bin = find_key(table, key);
  return bin->key == key && !bin->is_empty;
}
```

When you insert a key, there are three cases to consider. If the key is already in the table, you leave the counters alone. You also don't check if it is time to resize the table, since nothing has changed since the last update operation.

If you insert a key into an empty bin, you have one of two cases: the bin could be (an empty) part of a probe, in which case you have to increase the number of active bins but not the number of used bins—the bin was already in use, after all. Or, the bin could be outside a probe, in which case you need to increment both active and used.

Once you insert a key, you need to check if the load is more than half, and if it is, you grow the table to twice its current size.

```
void
insert_key(struct hash_table *table, unsigned int key)
{
  if (!contains_key(table, key)) {
    struct bin *key_bin = find_empty(table, key);

    table->active++;
    if (!key_bin->in_probe)
      table->used++; // We are using a new bin

    *key_bin = (struct bin){.in_probe = true, .is_empty =
    false, .key = key};

    if (table->used > table->size / 2)
      resize(table, table->size * 2);
  }
}
```

When deleting, you do nothing if the key is not already in the table. Otherwise, you remove it, and you have to decrease active and but not used, since the bin that contained the key is still in a probe. Then, you check if it is time to resize—if the load is less than 1/8 and the table is above its minimal size.

```
void
delete_key(struct hash_table *table, unsigned int key)
{
  struct bin *bin = find_key(table, key);
  if (bin->key != key)
    return; // Nothing more to do

  bin->is_empty = true; // Delete the bin
  table->active--;       // Same bins in use but one less active

  if (table->active < table->size / 8 && table->size >
  MIN_SIZE)
    resize(table, table->size / 2);
}
```

The resizing function is relatively simple since the real work is done in init_table(). You get hold of the old bin array, so you can copy bins and free memory. Then you call init_table() to update the table and allocate new bins, and in this call, you provide the range of old bins so init_table() can insert them. After that, you free the old array.

```
static void
resize(struct hash_table *table, unsigned int new_size)
{
  //Remember the old bins until we have moved them.
  struct bin *old_bins_begin = table->bins,
             *old_bins_end = old_bins_begin + table->size;
```

```
  // Update the table and copy the old active bins to it.
  init_table(table, new_size, old_bins_begin, old_bins_end);

  // Finally, free memory for old bins
  free(old_bins_begin);
}
```

The final function, init_table(), should also look mostly familiar. You allocate bins and initialize them as empty, just as in the previous chapter. Then you run through the old bins, and every time you see a non-empty bin, you use insert_key() to add them to the new table. Since the table is initialized with used = 0 and active = 0, inserting the keys this way takes care of the bookkeeping.

```
static void
init_table(struct hash_table *table, unsigned int size, struct
bin *begin,
            struct bin *end)
{
  // Initialize table members
  struct bin *bins = malloc(size * sizeof *bins);
  *table =
      (struct hash_table){.bins = bins, .size = size,
      .used = 0, .active = 0};

  // Initialize bins
  struct bin empty_bin = {.in_probe = false, .is_empty = true};
  for (unsigned int i = 0; i < table->size; i++) {
    table->bins[i] = empty_bin;
  }

  // Copy the old bins to the new table
  for (struct bin *bin = begin; bin != end; bin++) {
```

```
  if (!bin->is_empty) {
    insert_key(table, bin->key);
  }
 }
}
```

Theoretical Considerations for Choosing the Load Factor

You, somewhat arbitrarily, chose to grow or shrink the table when the load factor reached 1/2 or 1/8. In the amortized analysis of the running time, you saw that this gave you a linear running time for doing n insert or delete operations, but we didn't explore how the value of α affects this running time.

Now consider the general case of growing a table when the load factor reaches some α. The case for shrinking the table is similar: before you grew the table to size m, it had size $m/2$ and contained $\alpha m/2$ elements and $(1 - \alpha)m/2$ empty cells; see Figures 4-3 and 4-4. The next time you grow the table, you will have αm elements, so you must have inserted $\alpha m - \alpha m/2$ elements. The resizing then takes $2m$ operations, and you move αm elements to the new table. In total, you do $m(2\alpha + 2 - \alpha/2)$ operations, and you must pay for it in the $\alpha m - \alpha m/2$ insertion operations. Dividing one by the other, you get this:

$$\frac{m\left(2\alpha + 2 - \alpha/2\right)}{m\left(\alpha - \alpha/2\right)} = \frac{2\alpha + 2 - \alpha/2}{\alpha - \alpha/2}$$

This is the coefficient for the amortized line in the analysis for general α thresholds.

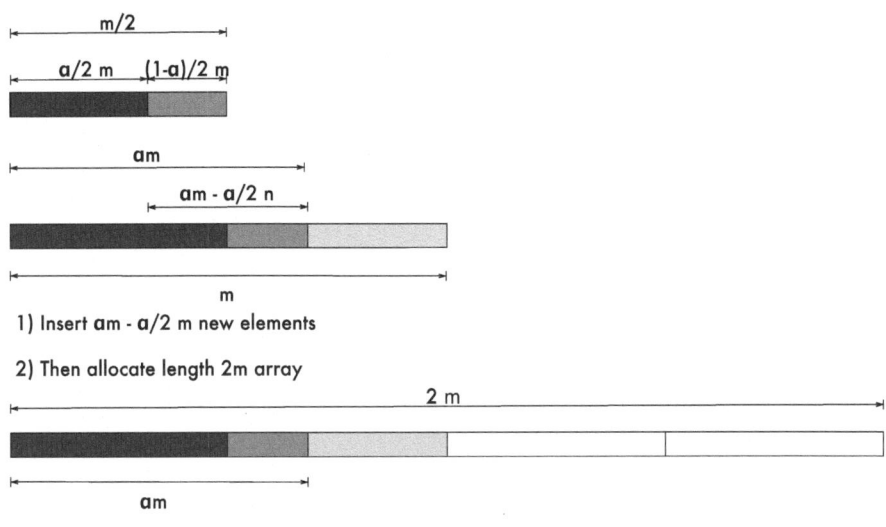

1) Insert $am - a/2\ m$ new elements

2) Then allocate length 2m array

3) And move an elements to the new array

Figure 4-3. *Resizing when you only fill the array up to αn elements before resizing*

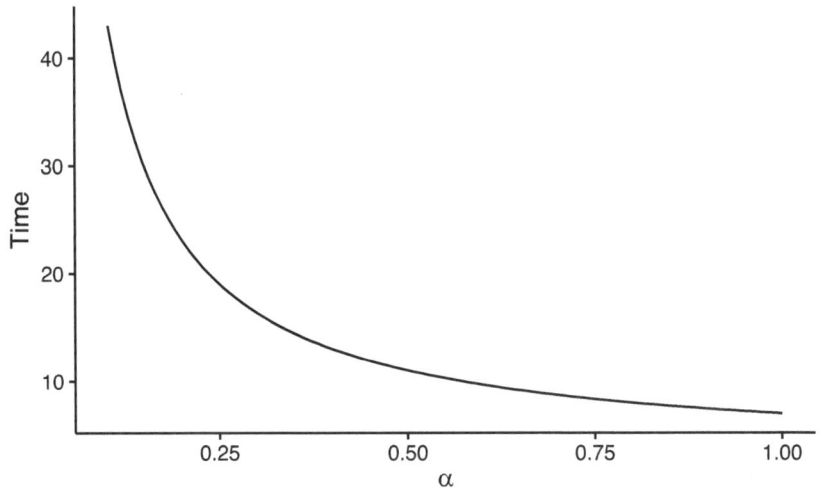

Figure 4-4. *The theoretical running time for growing a hash table, as a function of the load factor threshold, α*

In Figure 4-5, I plotted the theoretical running time for growing a table as a function of α. The figure implies that the higher the load, the better the performance. This shouldn't surprise you. The more you fill up the array before you resize, the less relative time you spend on the resizing. The figure is misleading, however. It does not take into account the costs of the probe operations, which also depend on the load factor. If you have an idea of how many successful and unsuccessful searches you expect in a typical run, you can combine this formulae with the formulae for probe lengths from the previous chapter, but it is easier to explore the actual running time via experiments.

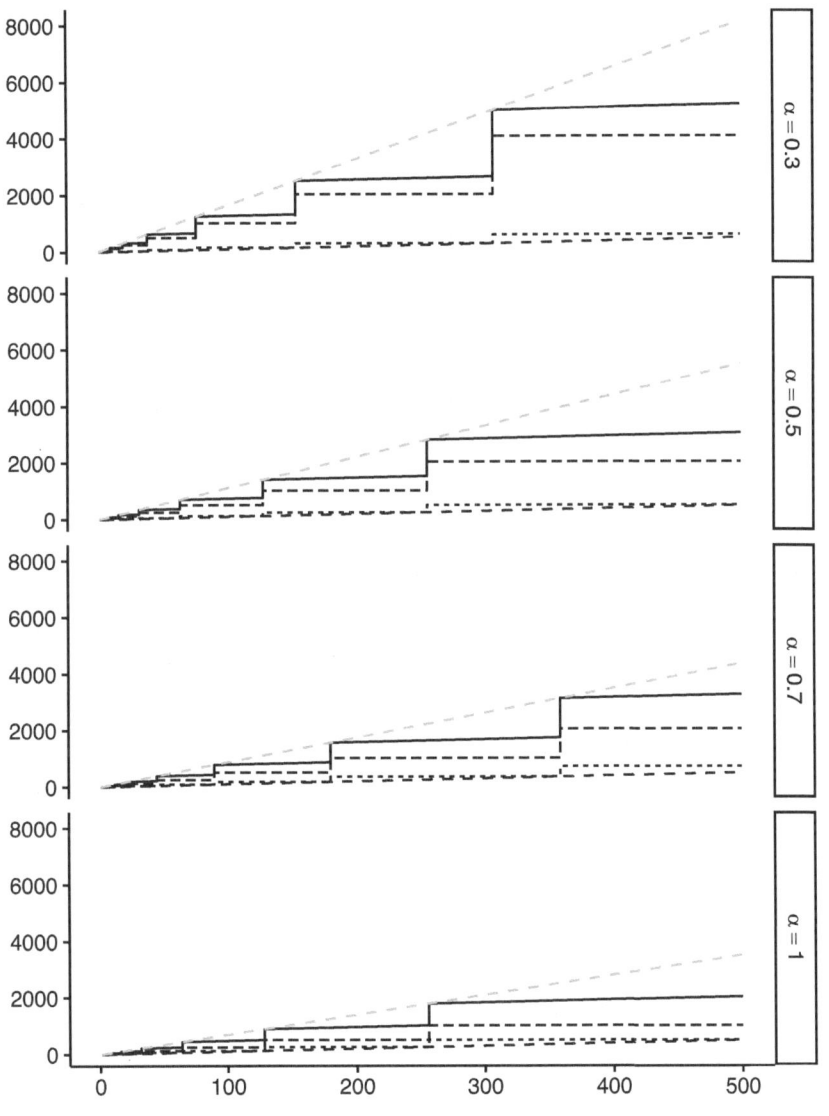

operations —— Total ···· Moves ––· Allocations – – Insertions

Figure 4-5. *The theoretical running time, split into its different components, for growing a hash table as a function of the load factor threshold, α*

Experiments

From the theoretical analysis of the performance of the hash tables with resizing, you should be able to insert n elements in time $O(n)$. You should also be able to test if these keys are in the table—they all should be—and do this test in linear time. You should be able to look up n random keys in linear time as well. This is a better measure of the actual performance since the running time guarantees are worse for keys that are not in the table compared to those that are. In either case, each lookup is in $O(1)$ if α is bounded by a constant. Finally, you should be able to delete the n keys stored in the table in time $O(n)$. Let's test this in practice.

Figure 4-6 shows the performance of the three different conflict resolution strategies when you insert, look up, and delete n elements while keeping the load factor $\alpha \leq 1/2$. Figure 4-7 shows the same experiments but contains only the open addressing strategies, using a different scale on the y-axis to make it easier to see their performance. In these experiments, I initialized all tables with size two. In a real application, you should consider the likely number of keys a table will hold. The table will adjust its size as needed, but if you know how many keys it will hold, you can save some time by initializing it with a capacity around that value.

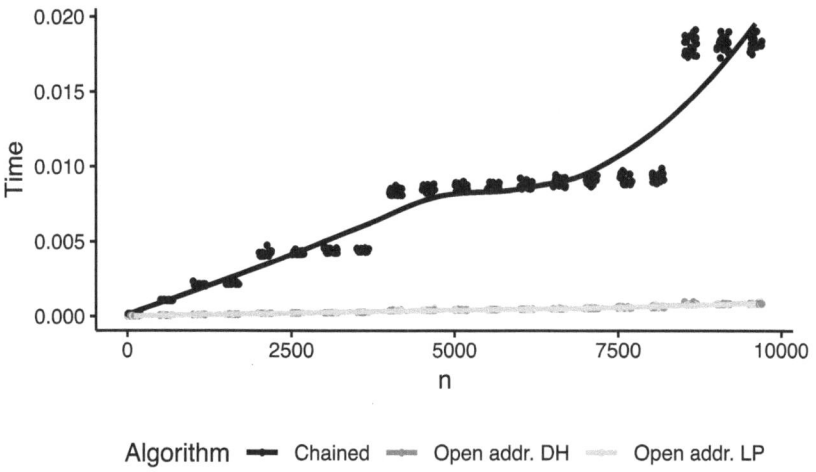

Figure 4-6. *Time usage for inserting n elements, looking them up, and then deleting them again, resizing along the way*

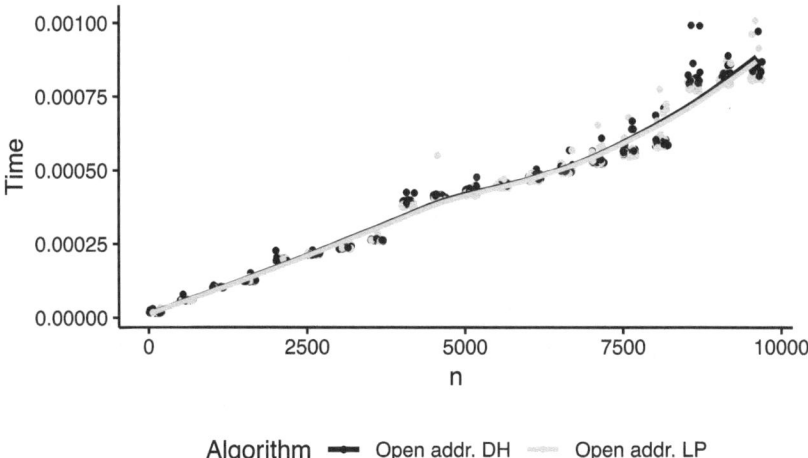

Figure 4-7. *Time usage experiments from Figure 4-6, including only the open addressing strategies*

The time usage looks more stepwise than linear, but considering that the amortized analysis only tells you that the time usage should be *bounded* by a line—and you know that resizing operations are expensive while non-resizing inserts and deletions are not—you shouldn't be surprised by this. The stepwise growth of the time usage measurements merely reflects the stepwise function of the smallest powers of two larger than n. Whenever $2^{k-1} < m \leq 2^k$, for some k, you have to allocate and initialize a table of size 2^k, and this table creation is the most expensive operation in the entire experiment. The steps you see in the experiments are the transitions between different powers of two.

As discussed in the previous section, the choice of the threshold for the load factor α can be any number $0 < \alpha < 1$. In Figure 4-8, you can see the performance of the same experiments as previously, with different choices of load factor limits. Figure 4-9 shows the same data (and a few more load factor limits) with smoothed curves, and in Figure 4-10, the same data is shown with selected load factors on the x-axis and the time on the y-axis.[2]

---

[2] For these experiments, I modified the resize thresholds in the code to resize at the specified load instead of at .

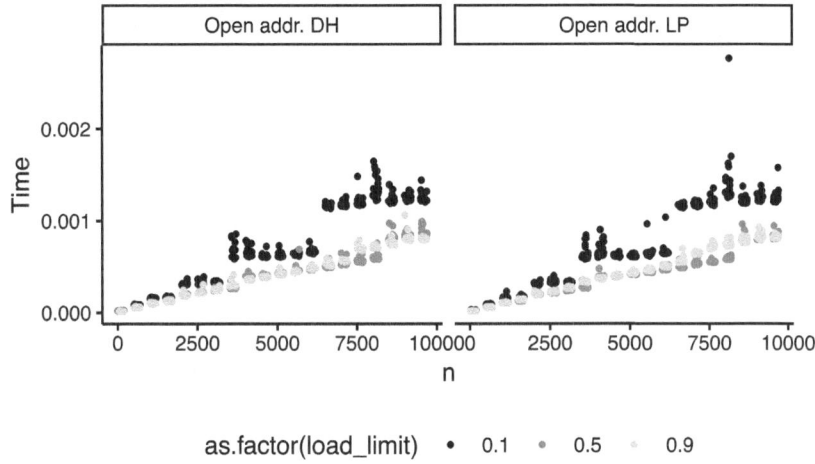

Figure 4-8. *Running time with different thresholds for resizing*

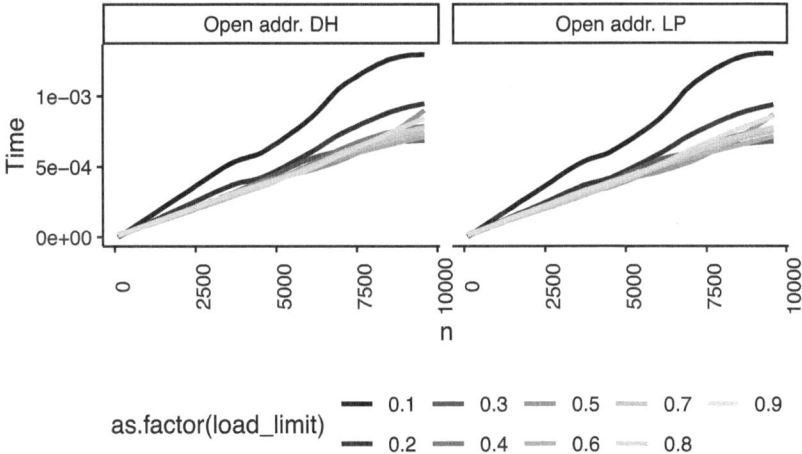

Figure 4-9. *Smoothed data from Figure 4-8*

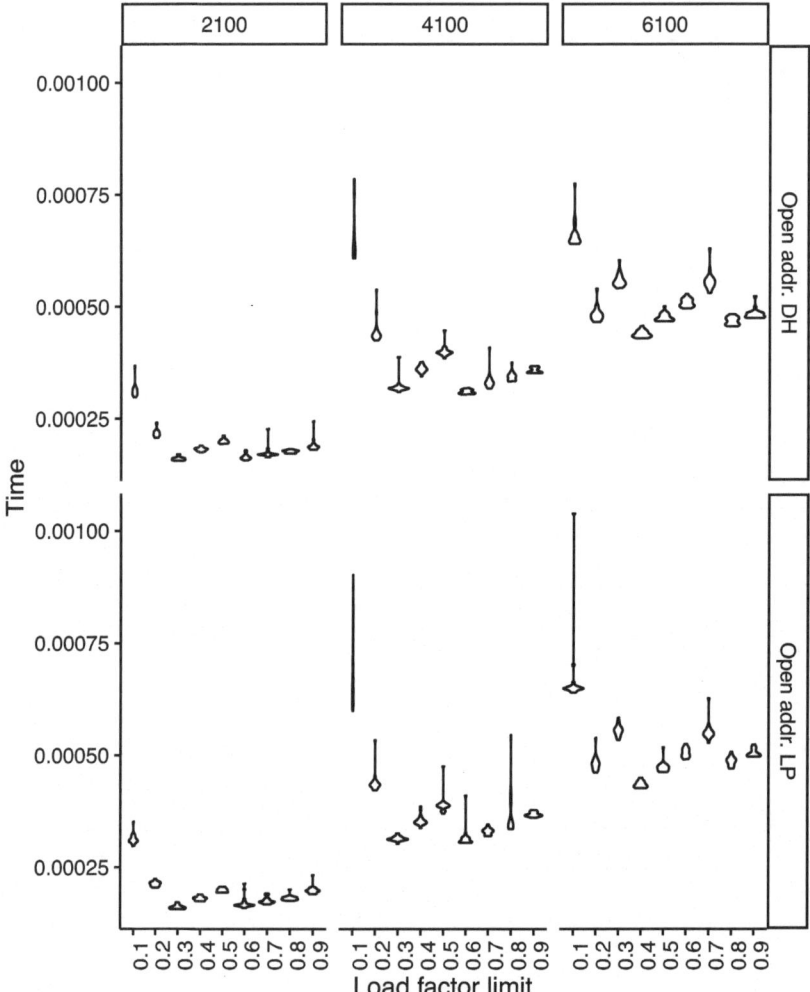

Figure 4-10. *Time as a function of n (the three panels) and different load factors*

You can see that the resize threshold affects the running time substantially. The tradeoff is between the cost of resizing versus the cost of probing as the load factor increases. If you set this threshold very low, you spend too much time resizing, while if you set it very high, you spend too much time probing.

The optimal choice of load factor threshold depends on your application, the typical sizes of n, and the insertion and deletion patterns. It also depends on your runtime system, which determines the cost of allocating m cells and setting them to 0. As a rule of thumb, though, you are generally best off if you make the threshold at least one-half. Less than that, and you always allocate at least twice as much memory as you need, potentially much more, if your threshold is small. The performance does not substantially degrade until you get close to a load factor of 1, so you will get better performance as your threshold approaches 1 than when it approaches 0. You will never do poorly with a threshold of around one-half. However, if you have an algorithm that crucially depends on the performance of a hash table, tweaking the threshold is a place to start in your algorithmic engineering.

Resizing When Table Sizes Are Not Powers of Two

You resize your hash table when it contains αm or $\alpha m/4$ elements, up or down, respectively, and you grow or shrink the table by a factor of two. As long as you use bit-masking to get the bin index for keys, you need the table size to be a factor of two. You can loosen that assumption if you use modulo, and then you can use a prime for m to avoid clustering of occupied bins.

Instead of growing and shrinking the table size in factors of two, you can introduce another parameter, β, and set the table size to $\beta \cdot m$ when growing and m/β when shrinking. Unfortunately, primes are not spread out such that p/β and βp will always be primes when p is, so you cannot achieve exactly this. The best you can do is pick primes that are close to this and tabulate primes p_1, p_2, ..., p_M (for some choice of M)[3] such that $p_{j-1} < p_j/\beta$ and $p_{j+1} > \beta \cdot p_j$.

To handle sizes and a table of primes, you can add a variable, primes_ idx, to your struct hash_table:[4]

```
struct hash_table {
  struct bin *bins;
  unsigned int size;
  unsigned int used;
  unsigned int active;
  unsigned int primes_idx; // <- new member
};
```

You can add a table of primes based on your choice of β. For example, for $\beta = 2$, you can define this table as so:

```
int primes[] = {
    2, 5, 11, 23, 47, 97, 197, 397,
    797, 1597, 3203, 6421, 12853, 25717, 51437,
    102877, 205759, 411527, 823117, 1646237,
    3292489, 6584983, 13169977 };
static unsigned int no_primes = sizeof(primes)/sizeof(int);
```

---

[3] Technically, you could compute these primes as needed, but this would be much slower than all the other hash table operations, so tabulating the primes you need is the only practical way. You can go to this URL, https://primes.utm.edu/ lists/, to get a list of the first 1,000, 10,000 or 50 million primes and build a table from them by filtering them according to your choice of step size.

[4] You do not necessarily need your table size to be prime just because you use modulo as a prime to get your bins. You can first get a random key using modulus and then mask out the lower bits. This way, you get a table size that is easier to work with—you can grow it and shrink it by a power of two—but, of course, at the cost of needing two operations to get your bin index. Since getting this index is unlikely to be the most time-critical when using a hash table, this is a small price to pay.

In insert_key, you can update the resizing code to this:

```
if (table->used > table->size / 2) {
    assert(table->primes_idx + 1 < no_primes);
    resize(table, table->primes_idx + 1);
}
```

And in delete_key, you can use this:

```
if (table->active < table->size / 8 && table->
primes_idx > 0) {
    resize(table, table->primes_idx - 1);
}
```

You can consider the theoretical amortized time analysis when you have a growth factor β added to the story. First, ignore α and assume you fill the table before you resize, similar to the growing array. The case is shown in Figure 4-11, and the reasoning is similar to what you did before to get the amortized running time. Between growing the array to size m and growing it to size βm, you must insert $m(1 - 1/\beta)$ elements. These elements must pay for the $m(1 - 1/\beta)$ insertions, then the allocation of an array of size βn, and finally for moving m elements to the new array. If you divide the total cost by the number of insertion operations, you get this:

$$\frac{m(2+\beta-1/\beta)}{m(1-1/\beta)}.$$

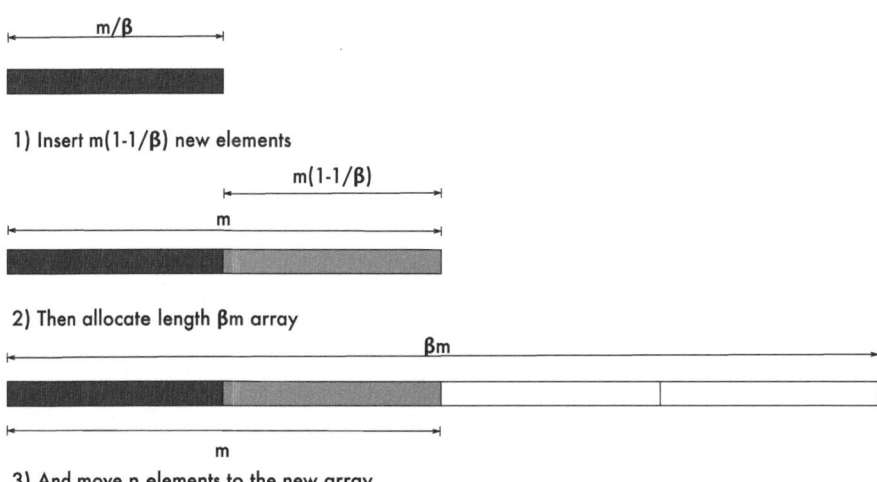

1) Insert m(1-1/β) new elements

2) Then allocate length βm array

3) And move n elements to the new array

Figure 4-11. *Growing an array by a factor of β*

Figure 4-12 shows this running time as a function of β while Figure 4-13 shows the components of the time usage for different values of β. When β is close to 0, you grow the array by a tiny amount each time you resize, and consequently, you have to reallocate memory frequently, which will give you a runtime penalty. When β grows to infinity, the running time degrades, simply because the cost of a single allocation will grow linearly in β.[5] The expression has a minimum at $\beta = 1 + \sqrt{2}$, shown as the black dot in the figure. Since $\beta = 1 + \sqrt{2} \approx 2.41$, your choice of β = 2 was not far from optimal, but could be better.

---

[5] The reason I say that n insertion takes (amortized) linear time is that the cost per operation does not depend on n. It does depend on β, however, as you see from the figure.

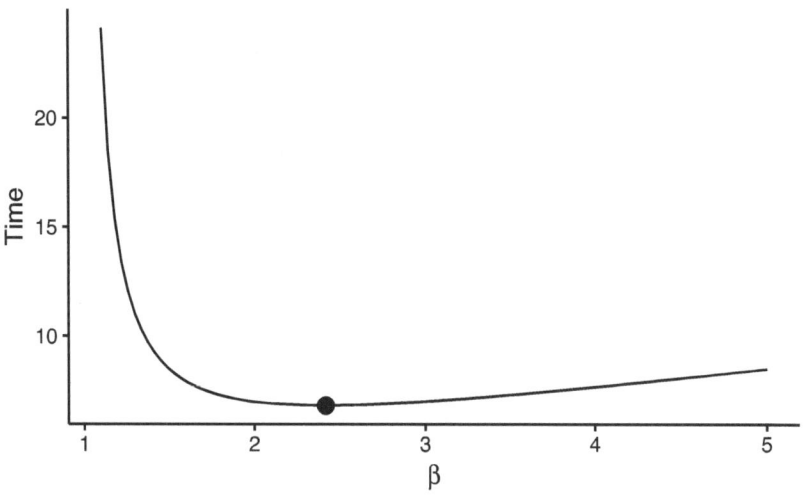

Figure 4-12. *Amortized running time for rescaling as a function of* β

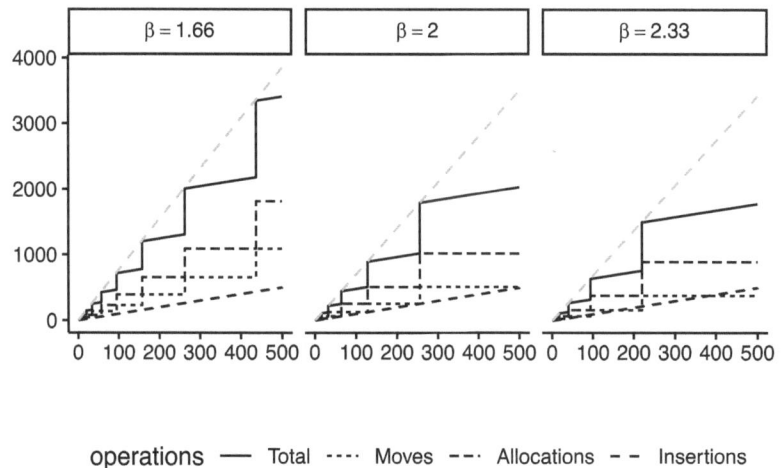

operations ——— Total ···· Moves ——· Allocations – – Insertions

Figure 4-13. *Details of the time usage when growing by a factor* β

Do not rely too much on this analytical result for the optimal choice of β, however. It assumes that all the operations you perform have precisely the same cost, which is unlikely to be true. The insertion cost depends on the price for updating linked lists or for probing the open addressing table;

the movement cost will depend on this cost as well. The allocation cost depends both on the operating and runtime system. You need experiments to get an accurate measurement of the performance in practice.

If you want your experiments to include open addressing, however, you cannot handle $\alpha = 1$, as you just did when you resized the table when it was full. So you need to add α to your analysis again. The full setup is shown in Figures 4-14 and 4-15. You derive the linear cost per insertion operation as before, just with $\alpha m - \alpha/\beta n$ insertions, allocation to a size βm array, and moving αn elements. The slope for the resulting line is as follows:

$$\frac{2\alpha + \beta - \alpha / \beta}{\alpha - \alpha / \beta}$$

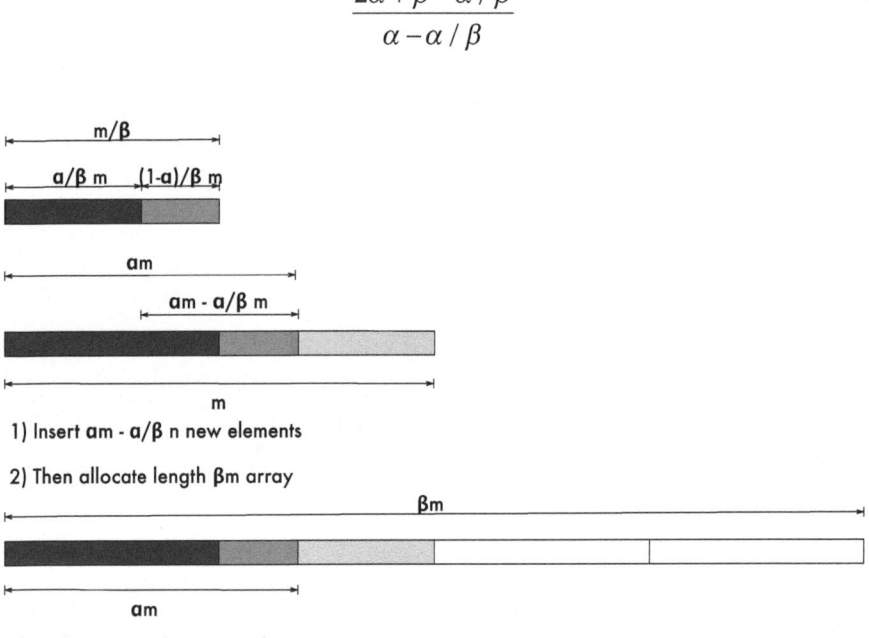

Figure 4-14. *Resizing when α and β are both taken into account*

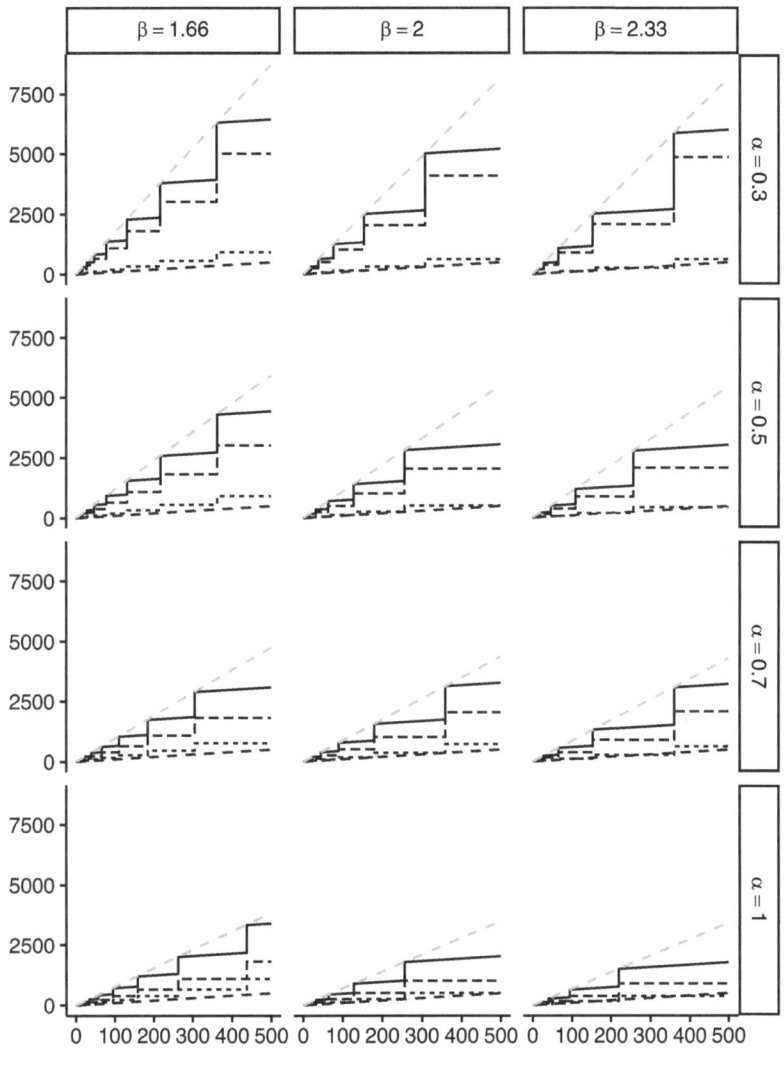

operations —— Total ···· Moves --· Allocations – – Insertions

Figure 4-15. *The different components of the running time for a growing table when α and β are both taken into account*

In Figure 4-16, I plotted this amortized operation cost as a function of both α and β. On the left, I show a range of α values for different choices of β. On the right, I show a range of β values for different choices of α. As discussed earlier, this formula suggests that you should always make α as large as possible, which you cannot do since you need to keep the load factor low. For any given choice of α, however, there is an optimal β at $1 - \sqrt{1+\alpha}$. This optimal value is shown as dots on the plot to the right. This optimum, however, requires that all operations take the same time, which they don't, so you have to use experiments to see how the actual running time varies for different choices of α and β.

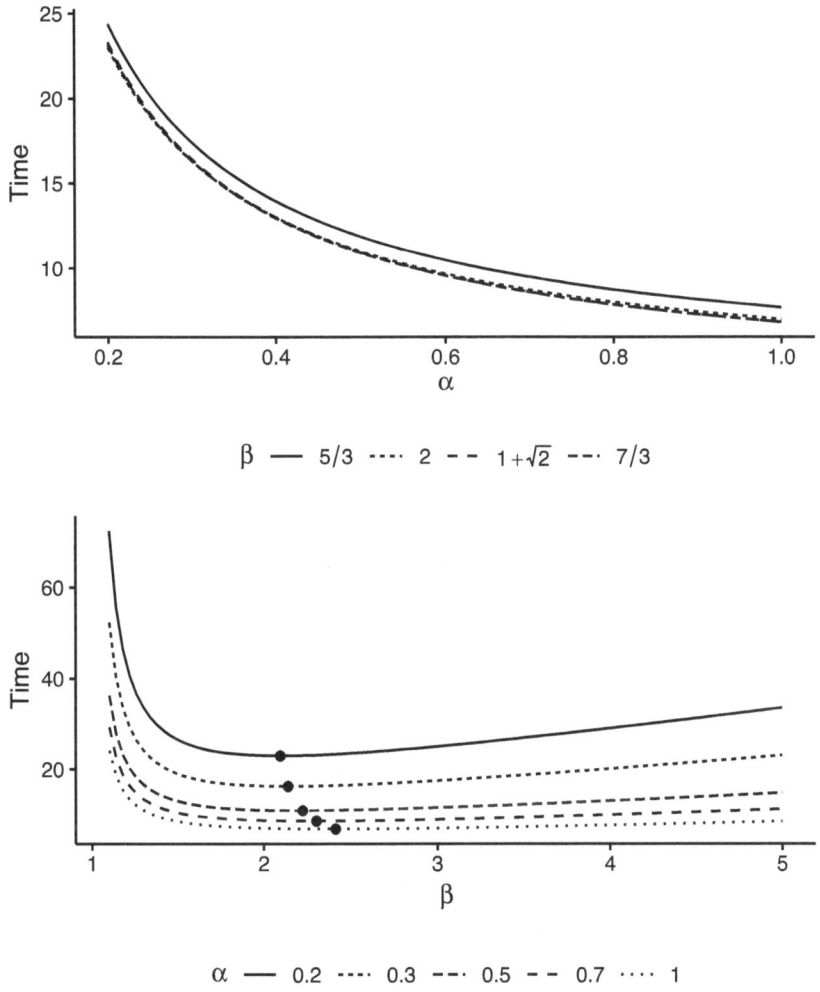

β —— 5/3 ···· 2 –– $1+\sqrt{2}$ ––· 7/3

α —— 0.2 ···· 0.3 ––· 0.5 –– 0.7 ···· 1

Figure 4-16. *Amortized operation cost when varying α and β*

In my experiments, using tables of sizes that are powers of two and
binning based on bit-masking performs better than tables of prime size
with modulus—see Figure 4-17—but this can vary. All measurements in
Figure 4-17 used linear probing. You saw that linear probing was slightly
superior to double hashing for the load-factor thresholds you used, so
you chose the fastest solution. You also did this to ensure that m and $h_2(k)$

are mutual primes and thus that the double hashing probe can scan the entire table. To guarantee this is trivial when m is a factor of two but more complicated otherwise.

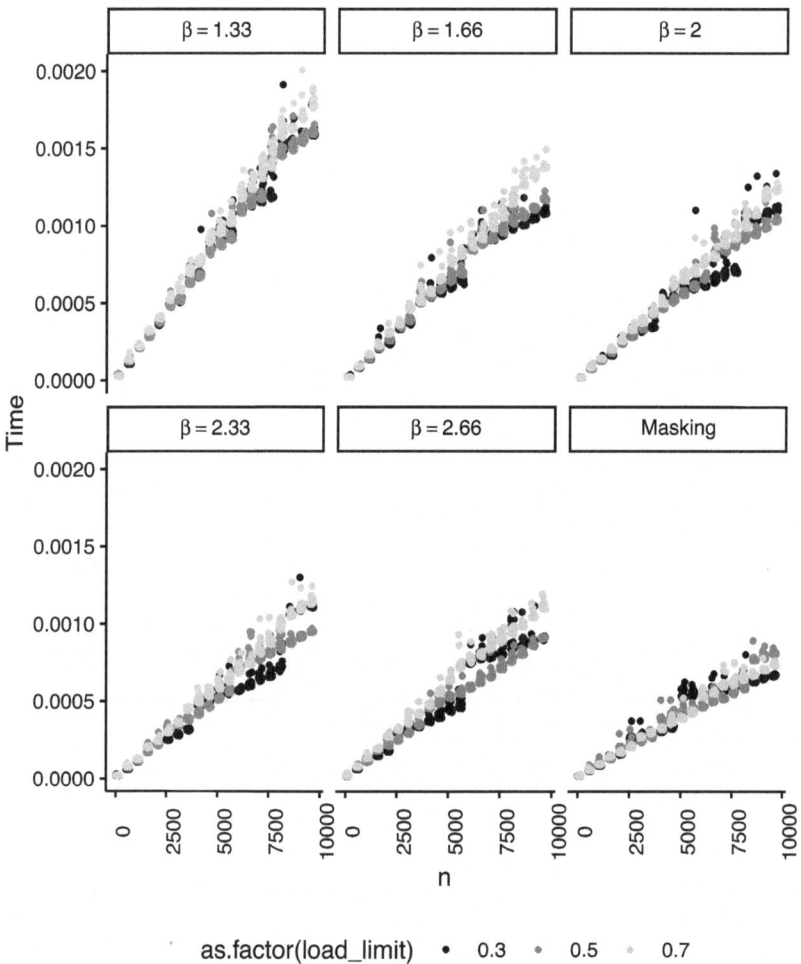

Figure 4-17. Time performance for tables of prime size with different choices of load factor thresholds, α, and resizing scales, β. Masking denotes the powers-of-two table with masking

Dynamic Resizing

Doubling and halving tables when you resize them gives you amortized constant time operations, but the resizing will be slow. This can be remedied by incrementally growing and shrinking a table, one bucket at a time. One approach to this is *linear hashing*[6] (not to be confused with linear probing for open addressing hashing). You still need the amortization trick to a much smaller degree, but you do not need to initialize tables when you resize.

The underlying idea is this: you split the keys into three parts, where the lower bits index into "sub-tables," the middle bits pick which sub-table a key should be inserted into, and the higher bits are ignored (for now). When you get a key, you mask out the lower bits to get an index that picks the sub-table and an index into the sub-table.

You then manipulate keys using bit operations as follows. Assume that sub-tables have size 2^s and that you have 2^t sub-tables. Then, given a key, you will mask out the lower s bits to get an index into a sub-table and use the following t bits to select a sub-table.

$$h_{bin}(x) = x \wedge (2^s - 1)$$

$$h_{tab}(x) = (x / 2^s) \wedge (2^t - 1)$$

Or in C:

```
h_bin = x & ((1 << s) - 1);
h_tab = (x >> s) & ((1 << t) - 1);
```

You then use h_tab to pick a sub-table and h_sub to get a bin index in the sub-table.

---

[6] Litwin, W. *Linear Hashing: A New Tool for File and Table Addressing.* Conference on Very Large Databases. (1980) pp. 212-223

For example, imagine that the key is eight bits, xxxxttbb, and the sub-table size is four (two bits). You would then mask out the four most significant bits, xxxx, use the next two to pick a sub-table, and the last two to select an entry into the sub-table:

```
// key = xxxx tt bb
bin = tables[tt][bb]
```

The bits you use to pick tables, tt here, will grow and shrink as you add and remove keys.

See Figure 4-18 for the basic idea of how to structure the table.

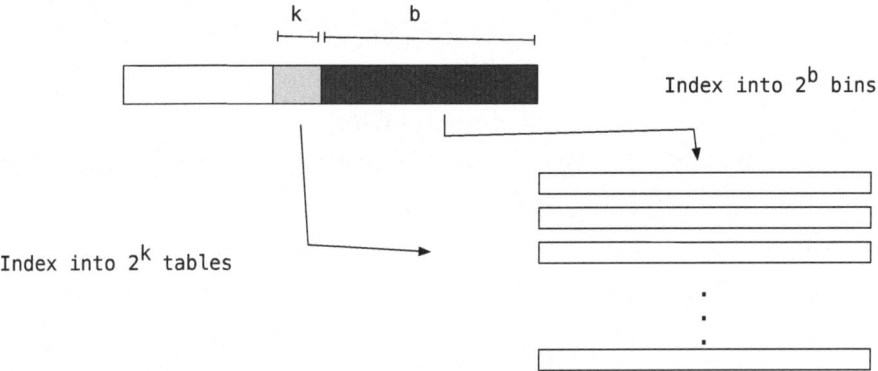

Figure 4-18. *Indexing keys*

You can map any number to table indices this way, and you will exploit the correspondence between bin indices and numbers in several places. Any time you have a table with N bins, any number in $[N]$ can be thought of as an index into a table of N bins or as two keys, a table and a sub-table index.

The resizing works by having a number $m = 2^b$, initially the size of a sub-table, and you have a variable split in the range 0, ..., m. As an invariant, all bins with index up to m + split - 1 will be initialized. When you insert a new key, you increment split and initialize the m + split bin. When you remove an element, you will clear the m + split - 1 bin and decrement split.

The growing and shrinking always involve moving elements from the range $0, ..., m - 1$ to the range $m, ..., 2m - 1$ (you will move elements from split to m + split). Shrinking involves moving elements from the range $m, ..., 2m - 1$ to the range $0, ..., m - 1$ (moving elements from m + split to split). Growing moves split to $2m$.

The way you should think about this is that the range $0, ..., m - 1$ is a table that uses one less "table bit" than the range $0, ..., 2m - 1$. As split moves from 0 to m, you conceptually add one bit to the table index. Keys that fall lower than split if you look only at the first b bits ($m = 2^b$), get to have one additional table bit, so they can fall in the range $0, ..., 2m - 1$ (although they only hit the range $0, ..., m$ + split because their lower b bits are less than split).

Every time split moves up, some keys get to use one additional bit. Likewise, when split moves down, some keys will get one less bit to index with.

Keys with the same b least significant bits might sit in different tables, but they will always sit at the same index into those tables. If the next k bits are the same, they will also be in the same table. But imagine if you extend the key by one additional bit, x_k. Then, the keys that would otherwise be in the same table at the same index, because they agree on the first k bits. They would sit in one of two tables, depending on which bit they have at position k. See Figure 4-19. If the keys are random, about half will sit in the first table and half in the second.

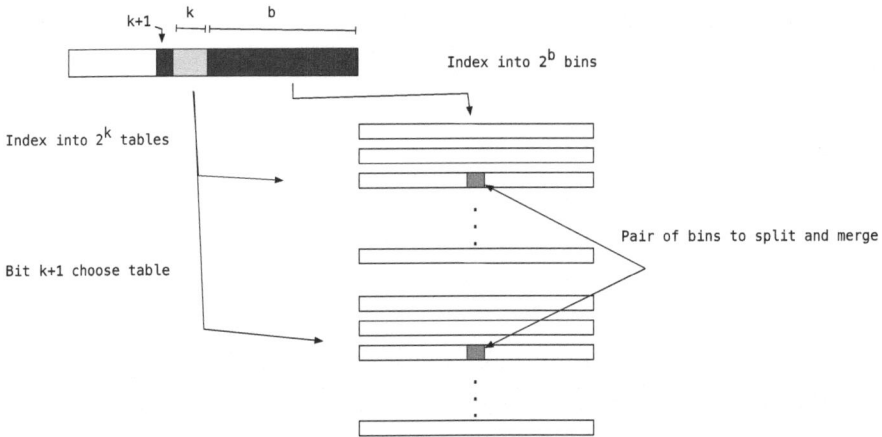

Figure 4-19. *Pairs of bins to split and merge*

This tells you that you can grow the table by splitting the split bin when you increase it, whereby "splitting" means looking at bin b and sending to the higher or lower index, split or $m + $ split, based on that bit. When you need to merge two bins, you mask out bit b and the $m + $ split and split bins end up in split.

If you grow and shrink a table you have allocated this way, you do not need to touch the sub-tables to double the size of the table. You need to allocate a new "table of tables", and you need to move pointers to the sub-tables to the new table, but this table is likely to be small compared to the total table size.

It is relatively simple to implement this idea with chained hashing because each bin when using k table bits only maps to two other bins when using $k + 1$ bits. The probing complicates initialization with open addressing. You can keep track of how much of a table is initialized by another counter if you use linear probing, but with double hashing, you either need to initialize tables when you allocate them, or you need to use complicated bookkeeping. I only present chained hashing in the following implementation.

I use this structure to hold the tables:

```
static const unsigned int SUBTABLE_BITS = 3; // 8 bins to a
sub-table

// A sub-table is an array of pointers to links.
// A sub-table plus an index is also a struct link **
// which by good fortune is a LIST.
typedef struct link **subtable;
struct hash_table {
  subtable *tables; // Tables is an array of sub-tables

  unsigned int table_bits; // Bits used for indexing into
                           sub-tables
  unsigned int split;      // Pointer to the bin you need to
                           split/merge

  unsigned int allocated_subtables; // Number of sub-tables
                                    allocated
};
```

You can set the number of bits you use per sub-table and the
SUBTABLE_BITS variable as you please, as long as it is non-zero. The
tables variable points to an array of sub-tables (and will still need the
amortization trick to grow). The table_bits variable is the number of
bits you have for tables, the split variable is the counter you use to index
where you need to split or merge, and allocated_subtables keeps track of
how many sub-tables you allocated so you can free them again.

You do not store m because you can get it from the existing
information. If you have s bits for sub-tables and t for tables, then m^{s+t}.

```
// Size of a word with `bits` bits
static inline unsigned int
bits_size(unsigned int bits)
```

```
{
  return 1 << bits;
}

// The range [0, split + m) are initialized.
// The range [split + m, 2m) is where we are
// adding new initialized bins through splitting.
static inline unsigned int
m(struct hash_table *table)
{
  return bits_size(table->table_bits + SUBTABLE_BITS);
}
```

The largest index currently active is at m + split, and you will need to access it later, so you must write a function for it:

```
// The largest bin that is currently in use
static inline unsigned int
max_index(struct hash_table *table)
{
  return m(table) + table->split;
}
```

For getting bin indices, there is a bit of bit-fiddling (no pun intended), but it can look like this:

```
// Mask for the lower `bits` bits
static inline unsigned int
bit_mask(unsigned int bits)
{
  return bits_size(bits) - 1;
}
```

```
// A mask for the parts of hash keys we are currently
considering
static inline unsigned int
key_mask(struct hash_table *table)
{
  return bit_mask(table->table_bits + 1 + SUBTABLE_BITS);
}

// The bins up to split + m are valid, the higher indices
   are not.
// If we are below this index, we can use the index,
   otherwise we need
// to use the smaller range [0, m).
static inline unsigned int
key_in_table_range(struct hash_table *table, unsigned int
hash_key)
{
  unsigned int masked_key = hash_key & key_mask(table);
  return (masked_key < max_index(table)) ? masked_key :
(masked_key - m(table));
}

static inline unsigned int
table_index(struct hash_table *table, unsigned int hash_key)
{
  return hash_key >> SUBTABLE_BITS;
}
static inline unsigned int
bin_index(struct hash_table *table, unsigned int hash_key)
{
  return hash_key & bit_mask(SUBTABLE_BITS);
}
```

```
// Get a bin from an index
static inline LIST
get_bin(struct hash_table *table, unsigned int hash_key)
{
  unsigned int tab_idx = table_index(table, hash_key);
  unsigned int bin_idx = bin_index(table, hash_key);
  return &table->tables[tab_idx][bin_idx];
}
```

Given a hash key, you mask out the lower $t + s + 1$ bits and check if you get a value in the range 0, ..., $m+$ split. If so, it is a valid index. If not, you have to use only the lower $t + s$ bits, or the number minus m. Once you have the correctly masked key, getting the table index and bin index is straightforward. It follows the previous example (except that you have already masked out the xxxx bits, so you don't need to do that again).

When you create a new table, you initialize m to the number of bins in a sub-table, you allocate an array of two sub-tables (but you only allocate and initialize the first), and you set the table bits and split to 0. This means you have m initialized bins that you can insert keys into.

```
struct hash_table *
new_table()
{
  struct hash_table *table = malloc(sizeof *table);

  // Initial size holds 2 table-pointers, [0,m) and [m,2m).
  table->tables = malloc(2 * sizeof *table->tables);

  // Allocate and initialize the first table only.
  table->tables[0] =
      malloc(bits_size(SUBTABLE_BITS) * sizeof
      *table->tables[0]);
```

```
  for (unsigned int i = 0; i < bits_size(SUBTABLE_BITS); i++) {
    table->tables[0][i] = NULL;
  }
  table->allocated_subtables = 1;

  table->table_bits = 0; // we only use bin bits initially
  table->split = 0;      // we start splitting at the first bin

  return table;
}
```

Deleting a table is not much different from the previous examples. The only complication is that you need to know how many sub-tables you have actually allocated, but you can keep track of that with the allocated_subtables variable, and then deallocating is a breeze.

```
void
delete_table(struct hash_table *table)
{
  // Delete lists in all initialized bins
  for (unsigned int bin = 0; bin < max_index(table); bin++) {
    free_list(get_bin(table, bin));
  }

  // Delete sub-tables.
  for (unsigned int tbl = 0; tbl < table->allocated_subtables;
  tbl++) {
    free(table->tables[tbl]);
  }

  // And finally free the tables array and the table
  free(table->tables);
  free(table);
}
```

The three operations you implement for all hash tables are straightforward as well. Whether you insert, check for membership, or delete a key, you get the appropriate bin (which involves the bit-masking) and then do roughly the same thing you did for all previous examples. The only real change is that you will do a split operation every time you insert and a merge operation every time you delete.

```
void
insert_key(struct hash_table *table, unsigned int key)
{
  LIST bin = get_bin(table, key_in_table_range(table, key));
  if (!contains_element(bin, key)) {
    add_element(bin, key);
    split(table);
  }
}

bool
contains_key(struct hash_table *table, unsigned int key)
{
  LIST bin = get_bin(table, key_in_table_range(table, key));
  return contains_element(bin, key);
}

void
delete_key(struct hash_table *table, unsigned int key)
{
  LIST bin = get_bin(table, key_in_table_range(table, key));
  if (contains_element(bin, key)) {
    delete_element(bin, key);
    merge(table);
  }
}
```

When you split, you need to prepare the new table at index $m +$ split and then split from index split to split and $m +$ split (max_index(table) in the C code).

```c
static void
split(struct hash_table *table)
{
  // Initialize the target bin at split + m.
  init_next_subtable(table);

  // Get the split bin and if there are elements there,
  // split them.
  LIST from_bin = get_bin(table, table->split);
  LIST to_bin = get_bin(table, max_index(table));
  split_bin(from_bin, to_bin, m(table));

  // Update counter to reflect that we have split
  table->split++;
}
```

Initializing the next table might involve allocating a new table, if you move from one sub-table to the next and the table there isn't already allocated. This will *also* involve growing the table->tables array if you are moving beyond its current range. The allocation and resizing is not something you haven't seen before, but you also have to increase the number of bits in table->table_bits if you grow the table->tables array, because this happens when split has reached m and you thus need more bits for the tables indices.

```c
void
init_next_subtable(struct hash_table *table)
{
  // Grow table if we have inserted m elements.
  if (table->split == m(table)) {
```

```
// Use one more bit for table indices
table->table_bits++;

// Alloc more table pointers (but don't initialize,
    we do that
// incrementally). The first half of the new size
    handles the
// new [0,m) and the second the new [m,2m) range. The
    new [0,m)
// range is already initialized.
size_t new_size = 2 * bits_size(table->table_bits) * sizeof
*table->tables;
table->tables = realloc(table->tables, new_size);

// Reset split pointer
table->split = 0;
}

unsigned int tab_index = table_index(table, max_
index(table));
if (tab_index == table->allocated_subtables) {
  // If we are moving into a new sub-table, we need to
      allocate it
  table->tables[tab_index] =
      malloc(bits_size(SUBTABLE_BITS) * sizeof
      *table->tables[tab_index]);
  table->allocated_subtables++;
  }
}
```

The actual split is the least exciting of the lot; it just involves running through a linked list and moving links—nothing you haven't done before either.

```
void
split_bin(LIST from_bin, LIST to_bin, unsigned int split_bit)
{
  struct link *link = *from_bin; // Catch list before we clear
                                      the bin.
  *to_bin = NULL;                 // Initialize if it
                                      isn't already
  *from_bin = NULL;               // Make bin ready for
                                      new values

  while (link) {
    struct link *next = link->next;
    if (link->key & split_bit) {
      // Move link
      link->next = *to_bin;
      *to_bin = link;
    } else {
      // Put link back into its current bin
      link->next = *from_bin;
      *from_bin = link;
    }
    link = next;
  }
}
```

When you merge, you decrement split, merge the bin in $m +$ split into the split bin and shrink the table if you have reduced the number of contained keys sufficiently.

```
static void
merge(struct hash_table *table)
{
```

```
// Decrement split. If it is a zero, we need to
// decrement table_bits and m instead, and set split
   to m - 1.
dec_split(table);

// Merge largest bin into split bin (well, one before the
   split bin so the
// indices match)
merge_bins(get_bin(table, max_index(table)), get_bin(table,
table->split));

shrink_tables(table);
}
```

Decrementing split is a little interesting. You cannot simply do split-- if split == 0. If split > 0 this will not be a problem, but when split is 0, you shouldn't decrement it (and get an underflow). Rather you should change $m \rightarrow m/2$ (by reducing table_bits). If you do reduce m, you need to set split to $m - 1$.

```
static inline void
dec_split(struct hash_table *table)
{
  if (table->split > 0) {
    table->split--;
  } else {
    table->table_bits--;
    table->split = m(table) - 1;
  }
}
```

Merging bins is also a simple linked list exercise:

```
static void
merge_bins(LIST from_bin, LIST to_bin)
{
  struct link *link = *from_bin;
  while (link) {
    struct link *next = link->next;
    link->next = *to_bin;
    *to_bin = link;
    link = next;
  }
}
```

Finally, shrinking the table is triggered when you reach a quarter of the allocated sub-tables. This is similar to what you did with the stack, which resembles the way you increase or decrease the capacity when you insert and remove keys. When you shrink the table, you need to free the sub-tables from the new size up to allocated_subtables and then update the table of tables and the allocated_subtables bookkeeping.

```
static void
shrink_tables(struct hash_table *table)
{
  // Checking when we point to the beginning of [0,2m).
    if (table->split == 0 &&
      bits_size(table->table_bits) < table->allocated_
      subtables / 4) {
    unsigned int new_no_tables = bits_size(table->table_
    bits + 1);
    for (unsigned int i = new_no_tables; i < table->allocated_
    subtables; i++) {
      free(table->tables[i]);
```

```
    }
    table->tables =
        realloc(table->tables, new_no_tables * sizeof
        *table->tables);
    table->allocated_subtables = new_no_tables;
  }
}
```

Incrementally growing and shrinking tables reduces the time it takes to resize, but all operations get more complicated and thus slower. Unless you want to reduce the time each operation takes, using more time on resizing and less on all the others is preferable. Over a series of operations, the latter will be faster.

CHAPTER 5

Adding Application Keys and Values

So far, the book has only considered storing integer keys in hash tables. Most of the techniques for implementing hash tables do not depend on whether you store simple keys or whether you associate application values with them. The setup where you only store keys that you can also use as hash keys, however, is practically never used in real-life applications. This chapter is about storing application values in bins together with their hash keys. You can download the code at `https://github.com/mailund/JoyChapter5`.

Hash tables are typically used for two things: to implement a *set* data structure or to implement a *map* data structure—the setup where you only store hash keys implements neither. What you've seen so far is implementations of sets of hash keys, but remember that you compute hash keys from some other data. Hash keys are the result of applying a hash function to the application keys, and they represent a simplification of the original data.

Implementing a set while storing hash keys alone does not guarantee that membership tests will work. It is likely to work since you expect different keys to map to the same key with a small probability, but you cannot rule out collisions. You will need to compare application keys when you search for membership or when you delete keys; only comparing hash keys will not suffice. Consider Figure 5-1. Note that you can have collisions at two levels. Different application keys can be mapped to the same hash key, and different hash keys can be mapped to the same table bin. This has solved the second problem; to solve the first, you need to store the application keys in the table.

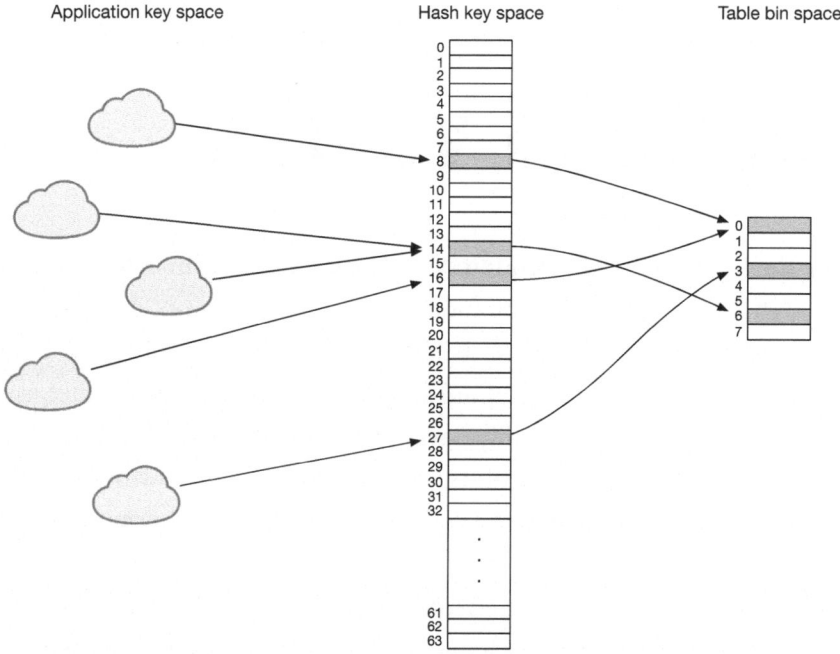

Figure 5-1. Hash keys and application keys

Theoretically, storing application keys and values in hash tables is not complicated. Instead of storing the hash key alone in links or bins, you store the application keys and, for maps, the application values. When you look up, you map the application key to a hash key, and then you proceed as you have done so far. In practice, however, and especially in C, it gets a bit more complicated. If you look up keys, how do you then compare keys? Do you need a callback function of some sort (like qsort or bsearch)? When you store anything in a data structure, you need to worry about ownership. Is the data structure expected to free its elements, or is the user? If the table is responsible for deleting elements, how do you configure this?

I do not explore all the issues with designing data structures in C, as that is beyond the scope of this book, but in this chapter, I present two approaches to implementing a generic hash table. I implement a generic hash set using macros to generate type-specific code, and I implement a hash map using callback functions. In both cases, I assume that the hash table takes ownership of all values you provide to it and will delete data when you no longer need it. This will not be the use pattern you want for all applications, but you should be able to adapt the two solutions to your needs if you want to.

In the first implementation, in the next section, I only store application keys in the table, but you sometimes want to store the hash keys as well, since recomputing hash keys can be expensive. This is an optimization, however, that I leave to the second implementation in this chapter.

Generating Hash Sets

For a hash set, you have some application type of keys, K, and from the hash table, you want operations for creating and destroying a table.

```
hash_table *new_table();
void free_table(hash_table *table);
```

The usual operations for updating and querying the hash table are as follows:

```
void insert_key(hash_table *table, K key);
void delete_key(hash_table *table, K key);
bool contains_key(hash_table *table, K key);
```

117

Translating this interface into the one you used in the previous chapters is easy in theory. You only need a function that can give you a hash key from a K key:

```
unsigned int hash(K key);
```

As already hinted at, things can be more complicated in C, because you can't use OOP techniques to implement comparisons of arbitrary types and you don't have destructors to handle when keys should be freed.

To use a generic key type, you must be able to compare two keys for equality, and you (probably) need a way to free keys. Together with the hash function, you could say that the key "interface" must satisfy:

```
unsigned int hash(K key);
bool eq(K k1, K k2);
void dealloc(K key);
```

And somehow, you must weave this interface into the hash table code.

In this chapter, you will generate type-specific tables, which means that given a type K and a specification of these three operations, you will generate a hash table for that key type. This resembles what languages that support generics do in this situation; it is just more cumbersome with C, where such generic programming is not natively supported.

The benefit of generics is that you can generate code that is optimized for the exact type you operate on without relying on function pointers that can slow down computation when your CPU cannot predict which branch you will jump to. In C, you can also get type-safe code, which isn't immediately available in the other generic approach you will use in the next section, which relies on void pointers to get generic functionality. The drawback of this type of generic programming is that C *really* doesn't support it, and you have to implement everything as code-generating macros.[1] Writing macros that generate code is tedious, error-prone, and hellish to debug. You have to be careful never to generate the same code twice unless you can link it separately—or you will have duplicated symbols, which the linker won't like. But it is a valid approach to generic data structures, and you will implement an example here that you can compare to the alternative approach in the next section.

Generic Lists

The hash table you will implement is a chained hashing table, so you will start with implementing generic lists, that is, lists that you can instantiate with any type K if you can provide the right operations for it. For lists, you don't need hashing, but you will need an equality and a deallocation operation. You will implement this macro:

```
GEN_LIST(LIST_NAME, KEY_TYPE, IS_EQ, FREE_KEY)
```

It generates a list called LIST_NAME (what this means will hopefully be clear shortly), with the underlying key type KE_TYPE (which would be your type K), and with macros or functions IS_EQ and FREE_KEY, which you can call to compare or free keys, respectively.

The macro needs to generate all the data structures you need plus all the operations you need (which for lists would be creation and destruction plus operations for adding, deleting, and querying a key). To avoid name clashes (or at least alleviate the headache that they might give you), you give the data structures a suffix and the functions a prefix derived from LIST_NAME. If you define a list with GEN_LIST(my_type, K, ...), you will get (among other things) a data structure called this:

```
struct my_type_list;
```

---

[1] I freely admit here that if I can avoid it, I never use this type of generated code. If I need generics, there are better macro languages than C's that you can use to instantiate code with different types. This book sticks to pure C.

And functions as so:

```
void my_type_add_key(struct my_type_list *, K key);
void my_type_delete_key(struct my_type_list *, K key);
bool my_type_contains_key(struct my_type_list *, K key);
void my_type_free_list(struct my_type_list *);
```

(There is no my_type_new_list here because you will initialize lists in a different way.)

Okay, that is the idea. Now, there are a few things to consider when implementing the idea. When you use macros to generate code, you are doing pure textural manipulation. The C preprocessor does not check that you are generating valid code, and it generally has no idea what the text is supposed to look like. So, you want to be careful when writing macros that are fairly easy to read. You will not get any help debugging the macros if they fail at some point. You also don't want the macros to have too many arguments or create too many types since that can be super difficult to debug as well. The simpler you can make the macros—even if this simplicity comes from exploiting type inference or instantiating macros that only exist to help you *write* macros—the better. You need a very simple design for linked lists so the macros that generate code for these lists are as short and simple as possible.

I will not dare to claim that I came up with the best and simplest solution here, but with a few design decisions on lists, I have written what I can consider fairly short macros for each generated function.

You learned about a few different approaches to linked lists earlier in the book, and the design here is not substantially different. You will need a link structure that holds data and some other structure, list, to represent complete lists. The representation I chose was this:

```
struct my_type_link {
  struct my_type_link *next;
  KEY_TYPE key;
};
```

```
struct my_type_list {
  struct my_type_link *head;
};
```

The true list is implemented as the links and the list structure contains a pointer to the head of the list. When you work with lists, they will be pointers to the list structure, not unlike the representation you had earlier of a pointer to a pointer of a link. This example does not abandon the pointer-to-pointer to link idea, though. You can implement most of the operations you need through an "iterator" interface, where an iterator is exactly a pointer-to-pointer to link.

Generating the structures is as simple as this macro:

```
#define GEN_LIST_STRUCTS(LIST_NAME, KEY_TYPE)  \
  struct LIST_NAME##_link {                     \
    struct LIST_NAME##_link *next;              \
    KEY_TYPE key;                               \
  };                                            \
  struct LIST_NAME##_list {                     \
    struct LIST_NAME##_link *head;              \
  };
```

If you have a struct my_type_list, that NULL can be assigned to any pointer type, so you don't need to generate constructors. If you define this:

```
#define NEW_LIST() { .head = NULL }
```

You can initialize a new list with this:

```
struct my_type_list list = NEW_LIST();
```

Now, to manipulate lists, you will define a few helper macros. The first,

```
#define LIST(LIST_NAME) struct LIST_NAME##_list
```

gives you a convenient way to get the name of the data structure you are generating from the macro argument LIST_NAME. The others give you a generic iterator interface into lists:

```
#define ITR(LIST) typeof(LIST->head) *

// Turn list into iter
#define ITR_BEG(LIST)  (&((LIST)->head))
// Check if you are at the end of the iteration
#define ITR_END(ITR)   (!*(ITR))
// Get next element in the iterator
#define ITR_NEXT(ITR)  (&((*(ITR))->next))
// Get the current iterator element
#define ITR_DEREF(ITR) (*(ITR))
```

The ITR(LIST) macro defines a type from a list. It uses the typeof() operator from C23, but if your compiler doesn't support it, you can replace it with this:

```
#define ITR(LIST_NAME) struct LIST_NAME##_link **
```

An iterator is just a pointer to a pointer to a link, as you have seen before. The ITR_BEG gives you an iterator that points to the head of a list (by dereferencing a pointer to a list and then getting the address of the head link).

```
struct my_type_list *list ...; // some list of my type
struct my_type_link *head = list->head; // head of the list
struct my_type_link **itr = &(list->head); // ITR_BEG(list)
```

The ITR_END macro tests if an iterator is pointing to NULL, which would be the end of a linked list, ITR_NEXT gets the next link in an iteration, and ITR_DEREF extracts the current link the iterator is referring to.

Going through pointers to pointers to links this way might seem complicated, but as you have seen before, it can simplify manipulating lists since you always have access to the pointers you need to update. The macros only give you a more convenient notation for manipulating lists in this way. But when you see the macros in action, you can judge for yourself.

Start by adding a key to a list:

```
#define PUSH_NEW_LINK(ITR)                              \
  do {                                                  \
    typeof(**ITR) *link = malloc(sizeof *link); \
    link->next = *(ITR);                                \
    *(ITR) = link;                                      \
  } while (0)

#define GEN_LIST_ADD_KEY(LIST_NAME, KEY_TYPE)       \
  void LIST_NAME##_add_key(LIST(LIST_NAME) * list, \
                           KEY_TYPE key)            \
  {                                                 \
    PUSH_NEW_LINK(ITR_BEG(list));                   \
    ITR_DEREF(ITR_BEG(list))->key = key;            \
  }
```

The GEN_LIST_ADD_KEY macro generates a function. The function name is the concatenate of LIST_NAME and _add_key, so if you had called the macro GEN_LIST_ADD_KEY(my_type, char *) for example, you would get this function:

```
void my_type_add_key(struct my_type_list *list, char *key);
```

The PUSH_NEW_LINK macro allocates a new link, points its next pointer at the link the iterator is pointing to, and then writes the address of the new link into the iterator. In effect, it pushes the new link to the front of the list that ITR is pointing at. Again, if your compiler does not yet support typeof(), you can generate the iterator type from LIST_NAME. The function you generate with GEN_LIST_ADD_KEY will, in its body, contain the expanded PUSH_NEW_LINK that will put a new link at the front of the list, and then the ITR_DEREF(ITR_BEG(list))->key = key will write the key into this new link. (The ITR_DEREF(ITR_BEG(...)) to get the head element in the list is something you would never write if you were implementing the function directly—there you could just write list->head->key, but I prefer to keep the macro operations small so I can keep track of them, and if that means I have to write something with operations I normally wouldn't, then so be it. The generated code will amount to the same thing.)

This macro only needs to know the name you gave the list, LIST_NAME, and the type of keys, KEY_TYPE, because the function you generate needs to know the type.

To free an entire list, you also need to know how to free keys, so that macro will take an additional FREE_KEY argument.

```
#define DELETE_LINK(ITR)                          \
  do {                                            \
    typeof(**ITR) *next = (*(ITR))->next;  \
    free(*(ITR));                                 \
    *(ITR) = next;                                \
  } while (0)

#define GEN_LIST_FREE_LIST(LIST_NAME, KEY_TYPE, FREE_KEY) \
  void LIST_NAME##_free_list(LIST(LIST_NAME) * list)      \
  {                                                        \
    ITR(list) itr = ITR_BEG(list);                         \
    while (!ITR_END(itr)) {                                \
      FREE_KEY(ITR_DEREF(itr)->key);                       \
      DELETE_LINK(itr);                                    \
    }                                                      \
  }
```

The DELETE_LINK macro generates code for freeing the front link an iterator is pointing at. You get hold of the iterator's next in a temporary variable next, free the link the iterator points to, and then point ITR to next. The GEN_LIST_FREE_LIST macro generates a LIST_NAME##_free_list function that takes a list as an argument; that function will get the head of the list and free links as long as the head is not NULL. Before you free a link, you dereference the iterator to get the link; from there, you get the key, and you call FREE_KEY to free the application key.

To check if a list contains a key, you only need IS_EQ and you can use the iterators to run through a list and dereference them to get access to keys. You can compare the keys to the one you are searching for by calling IS_EQ and then report what you find:

```
#define GEN_LIST_CONTAINS_KEY(LIST_NAME, KEY_TYPE, IS_EQ) \
  bool LIST_NAME##_contains_key(LIST(LIST_NAME) * list,    \
                                const KEY_TYPE key)         \
  {                                                         \
    for (ITR(list) itr = ITR_BEG(list);                    \
         !ITR_END(itr);                                     \
         itr = ITR_NEXT(itr)) {                             \
      if (IS_EQ(ITR_DEREF(itr)->key, key)) {                \
        return true;                                        \
      }                                                     \
    }                                                       \
    return false;                                           \
  }
```

To delete a specific key, you need to compare and free keys, so for this macro, you need both IS_EQ and FREE_KEY:

```
#define GEN_LIST_DELETE_KEY(LIST_NAME, KEY_TYPE, IS_EQ, FREE_KEY) \
  void LIST_NAME##_delete_key(LIST(LIST_NAME) * list,              \
                              const KEY_TYPE key)                  \
```

125

```
{                                                            \
  for (ITR(list) itr = ITR_BEG(list);                        \
       !ITR_END(itr);                                        \
       itr = ITR_NEXT(itr)) {                                \
    if (IS_EQ(ITR_DEREF(itr)->key, key)) {                   \
      FREE_KEY(ITR_DEREF(itr)->key);                         \
      DELETE_LINK(itr);                                      \
      return;                                                \
    }                                                        \
  }                                                          \
}
```

In the function generated here, you use the iterators for a linear scan through the linked list, use the IS_EQ on each key you see to determine if you have found the key you are looking for, and if you have, you use FREE_KEY to delete the key and DELETE_LINK to remove the link. If this wasn't a function-generating macro but a regular function, I doubt there would be anything to confuse readers here. (If there is when you are reading the macros, I hear you. Code-generating macros can be a headache.)

The complete code-generating macro is simply the combination of all the macros you wrote:

```
#define GEN_LIST(LIST_NAME, KEY_TYPE, IS_EQ, FREE_KEY)          \
  GEN_LIST_STRUCTS(LIST_NAME, KEY_TYPE);                         \
  GEN_LIST_ADD_KEY(LIST_NAME, KEY_TYPE);                         \
  GEN_LIST_DELETE_KEY(LIST_NAME, KEY_TYPE, IS_EQ, FREE_KEY); \
  GEN_LIST_CONTAINS_KEY(LIST_NAME, KEY_TYPE, IS_EQ);            \
  GEN_LIST_FREE_LIST(LIST_NAME, KEY_TYPE, FREE_KEY);
```

To generate code, you only have to provide the list name, the underlying type, and the two operators IS_EQ and FREE_KEY. These can be macros or functions.

For example, if you want lists of integers, the appropriate comparison is just ==, and you don't need to free them, as they will be embedded in the links you are already freeing in the list code. So, you could define an integer linked list like this:

```
#define EQ_CMP(A, B) ((A) == (B))
#define NOP_DESTRUCTOR(KEY) //

GEN_LIST(integer,        // name of the list type
         unsigned int,   // underlying type
         EQ_CMP,         // how you compare keys
         NOP_DESTRUCTOR) // how you free keys;
```

If you instead work with pointers to integers, you should dereference them before you compare them, and you probably need to call free on them when they are deleted:

```
#define DEREF_EQ_CMP(A, B) (*(A) == *(B))
GEN_LIST(intp, unsigned int *, DEREF_EQ_CMP, free);
```

For strings, you would also free them, but the comparison would probably be testing if strcmp() returned 0:

```
#define STR_EQ(A, B) (strcmp(A, B) == 0)
GEN_LIST(str, char *, STR_EQ, free);
```

Generating a Hash Set

With a chained hashing strategy, you handle most of the operations in linked lists, so you do not have much more to generate to also get a hash set. But you have to be careful with the names you give functions so they don't clash. You can write some macros to assign names to things:

```
#define BIN(HASH_NAME) struct HASH_NAME##_bin_list
#define HTABLE(HASH_NAME) struct HASH_NAME##_hash_table
```

```
#define LIST_FN(HASH_NAME, FUNC_NAME) HASH_NAME##_
bin##_##FUNC_NAME
#define HASH_FN(HASH_NAME, FUNC_NAME) HASH_NAME##_##FUNC_NAME
```

Here, HASH_NAME is the name that defines hash structures and functions, and you define a derived name BIN(HASH_NAME) for the linked lists. This is the name you will use when you generate code for the lists. The HTABLE(HASH_NAME) will then be the corresponding name for hash table code. Finally, you use LIST_FN and HASH_FN to get the generated names for functions from the lists and hash tables, respectively.

You also define a minimum size for hash tables:

```
#define MIN_SIZE 8
```

This is the same as you saw in Chapter 4.

When you generate structures, you generate the linked list code first, with the comparison and destructor operations appropriate for the key type (is is in the lists these are used, after all), and then you generate a hash table structure. The latter will have an array of lists—represented as a pointer to BIN(HASH_NAME)—and the size and used counters you used in the previous chapter.

```
#define GEN_HASH_STRUCTS(HASH_NAME, KEY_TYPE, KEY_CMP, KEY_
DESTRUCTOR) \
GEN_LIST(HASH_NAME##_bin, KEY_TYPE, KEY_CMP, KEY_DESTRUCTOR) \
HTABLE(HASH_NAME) {          \
  BIN(HASH_NAME) * bins;  \
  unsigned int size;       \
  unsigned int used;       \
};
```

The code you generate to create and free tables is close to the code you used in Chapter 4. I inlined a few things to generate fewer functions, but you should see the resemblance. In the creation code, you allocate the table structure and the bins, run through the bins, and initialize them with NULL for their head.

```
#define GEN_NEW_TABLE(HASH_NAME)                                  \
  HTABLE(HASH_NAME) * HASH_FN(HASH_NAME, new_table)()             \
  {                                                               \
    HTABLE(HASH_NAME) *table = malloc(sizeof *table);             \
    BIN(HASH_NAME) *bins = malloc(MIN_SIZE * sizeof *bins);       \
    *table = (HTABLE(HASH_NAME)){.bins = bins,                    \
                                 .size = MIN_SIZE,                \
                                 .used = 0};                      \
    for (BIN(HASH_NAME) *bin = table->bins;                       \
         bin < table->bins + table->size;                         \
         bin++) {                                                 \
      bin->head = NULL;                                           \
    }                                                             \
    return table;                                                 \
  }
```

When you delete, you call the list's free_list function (using LIST_FN(HASH_NAME, free_list) to get the right name). It will take care of freeing the application keys.

```
#define GEN_FREE_TABLE(HASH_NAME)                                 \
void HASH_FN(HASH_NAME, free_table)(HTABLE(HASH_NAME) *table)\
{                                                          \
  for (BIN(HASH_NAME) *bin = table->bins; \
       bin < table->bins + table->size;   \
       bin++) {                           \
    LIST_FN(HASH_NAME, free_list)(bin);   \
  }                                       \
```

```
  free(table->bins);                          \
  free(table);                                \
}
```

As before, you want a function that gives you a bin (i.e., a linked list) from a hash key:

```
#define GEN_GET_KEY_BIN(HASH_NAME)                          \
  BIN(HASH_NAME) *                                          \
  HASH_FN(HASH_NAME, get_key_bin)(HTABLE(HASH_NAME) *table, \
                                  unsigned int hash_key)    \
  {                                                         \
    unsigned int mask = table->size - 1;                    \
    unsigned int index = hash_key & mask;                   \
    return &table->bins[index];                             \
  }
```

Generating a function for this operation is not what I would have preferred since it pollutes the namespace just for convenience, but statement expressions are not yet part of the C standard, so a function it is.

With this function, adding keys, deleting keys, and checking for keys are very similar to what you had before, even though the syntax is more complicated because you need to track the generated names. The only main difference between what you saw in Chapter 4 is that you need to translate application keys to hash keys before you can call the (generated) get_key_bin, so you need the HASH operation as a parameter to the macros, and you need to call it on the application key to get the hash key.

```
#define GEN_INSERT_KEY(HASH_NAME, KEY_TYPE, HASH)             \
  void                                                        \
  HASH_FN(HASH_NAME, insert_key)(HTABLE(HASH_NAME) *table,    \
                                 KEY_TYPE key)                \
  {                                                           \
    BIN(HASH_NAME) *bin =                                     \
```

```
      HASH_FN(HASH_NAME, get_key_bin)(table, HASH(key));    \
    if (!LIST_FN(HASH_NAME, contains_key)(bin, key)) {       \
      LIST_FN(HASH_NAME, add_key)(bin, key);                 \
      table->used++;                                         \
      if (table->size == table->used) {                      \
        HASH_FN(HASH_NAME, resize)(table, 2*table->size);    \
      }                                                      \
    }                                                        \
  }

#define GEN_CONTAINS_KEY(HASH_NAME, KEY_TYPE, HASH)           \
  bool                                                       \
  HASH_FN(HASH_NAME, contains_key)(HTABLE(HASH_NAME) *table, \
                           KEY_TYPE key)                      \
  {                                                          \
    BIN(HASH_NAME) *bin =                                    \
        HASH_FN(HASH_NAME, get_key_bin)(table, HASH(key));   \
    return LIST_FN(HASH_NAME, contains_key)(bin, key);       \
  }

#define GEN_DELETE_KEY(HASH_NAME, KEY_TYPE, HASH)             \
  void                                                       \
  HASH_FN(HASH_NAME, delete_key)(HTABLE(HASH_NAME) *table,   \
                           KEY_TYPE key)                      \
  {                                                          \
    BIN(HASH_NAME) *bin =                                    \
      HASH_FN(HASH_NAME, get_key_bin)(table, HASH(key));     \
    if (LIST_FN(HASH_NAME, contains_key)(bin, key)) {        \
      LIST_FN(HASH_NAME, delete_key)(bin, key);              \
      table->used--;                                         \
      if (table->size > MIN_SIZE                             \
          && table->used < table->size / 4) {                \
```

131

```
      HASH_FN(HASH_NAME, resize)(table, table->size / 2); \
    }                                                      \
  }                                                        \
}
```

The only remaining function is `resize`. Here, I changed the code a
little. Instead of having a `copy_links` function, I have inlined the code—to
avoid generating more functions than I have to, thereby alleviating the
risks of name clashes—and instead I used a macro that moves a link from
one list iterator to another. I also need to compute the hash keys to get the
bins I move the values to. If I had stored the hash keys in the lists—like I
will in the structure in the next section—I could have reused the computed
value instead.

```
#define MOVE_LINK(FROM, TO)                    \
  do {                                         \
    typeof(**FROM) *link = *FROM;              \
    *FROM = link->next;                        \
    link->next = *TO;                          \
    *TO = link;                                \
  } while (0)

#define GEN_RESIZE(HASH_NAME, HASH)                        \
  void                                                     \
  HASH_FN(HASH_NAME, resize)(HTABLE(HASH_NAME) *table,     \
                             unsigned int new_size)        \
  {                                                        \
    BIN(HASH_NAME) *old_bins = table->bins,                \
                   *old_from = old_bins,                   \
                   *old_to = old_from + table->size;       \
    table->bins = malloc(new_size * sizeof *table->bins);  \
    table->size = new_size;                                \
    for (BIN(HASH_NAME) *bin = table->bins;                \
```

```
      bin < table->bins + table->size;                    \
      bin++) {                                             \
    bin->head = NULL;                                      \
  }                                                        \

  for (BIN(HASH_NAME) *bin = old_from;                     \
       bin < old_to;                                       \
       bin++) {                                            \
    for (ITR(bin) itr = ITR_BEG(bin); !ITR_END(itr);) {  \
      unsigned int hash_key = HASH(ITR_DEREF(itr)->key); \
      MOVE_LINK(itr,                                       \
          ITR_BEG(HASH_FN(HASH_NAME, get_key_bin)(table, hash_
          key))); \
    }                                                      \
  }                                                        \
  free(old_bins);                                          \
}
```

With this kind of generated code, you can emulate the generics found
in many other languages. Writing code-generating macros is far from easy,
and using the generated code isn't necessarily easy either. In the code I
presented, I generate structures and functions as one unit, but this will not
work across compilation units where the linker cannot handle duplication
of symbols. There, you need to use a macro that generates structures
and prototypes and another that generates the functions. But even with
that approach, there are drawbacks. You get (binary) copies of the code
for each instantiation, leading to binary bloat. If you get complication
errors, tracking them from the generated code into the macros you used to
generate them is often far from trivial. While generating code is sometimes
the right approach and often leads to more efficient code, writing generic
code directly in C is sometimes the better choice. And that is what you will
do now, for a hash map.

Hash Maps

This section shows you how to implement hash maps using an alternative approach to writing generic hash tables in C. In this section, you do not generate code, so you have to rely on the one generic type that the C language has: the void pointer. The language standard guarantees that a variable of type void * can be assigned any pointer type and that any pointer type variable can be assigned a void *. This means that you can write code that uses void * objects, and this code can handle any other type of pointers.

A drawback is that type checking variables mostly goes out the window—you can assign an int * to a void * and then to a char * without type issues (but likely with substantial runtime issues). You can get around this by writing wrapper code with the correct pointer types, and you can use techniques similar to those in the previous section to auto-generate such wrappers. If you do, you will avoid many of the drawbacks of the generated code. The main code is the same for all instances of tables because you use the underlying void * types instead of generating tables for each type, and the generated code can typically be inlined so an optimizing compiler can get rid of it after checking type correctness. I don't generate such wrapper code here, but I trust you can easily do so based on what you learned in the previous section.

Another drawback is more substantial for the ergonomics of the code and difficult to get around. The approach can *only* work on pointers. You cannot assign an int or a char in a void * (at least not according to the C standard). For many types, this results in some cumbersome code. Say, for example, you want a map of strings to integers. Strings are already pointers, char *, so those are not a problem, but any integer you have, you must translate into an int *. If you have a variable i, you can use &i, but for a literal, like 42, you need tricks like &(int){42}). For example:

```
int i = 13;
add_map(map, "foo", &i);            // maps foo -> 13
add_map(map, "bar", &(int){42}); // maps bar -> 42

int j = *(int *)lookup_key(map, "bar"); // gets us 42
printf("j = %d\n", j);
```

In both cases, you *must* ensure that nothing in the value you insert into the table isn't changed or the hash mechanics cannot find them again. That means you cannot assign to i again if the pointer is inserted verbatim, and likely, you cannot create another &(int){literal} expression again, as compilers tend to reuse their memory. Of course, this is simply part of a larger problem when working with pointers; if you have pointers to data, you can modify it, and if you have data in a hash table, you absolutely must not do so. It is just easier to get it wrong with expressions like these.

The hash tables you create will be able to handle expressions like these, but they require some pointer discipline. You can't get around working with pointers, as that is all that void * can handle, but you can make it as flexible and as easy to use as that constraint allows. It comes at a performance cost, and you can get around some of it by modifying the code to your needs. Essentially, the rule is that everything in a table is owned by the table, so the table must copy keys and values when you insert them into it. In many cases, this is unnecessary (and to some degree, you can also avoid it with the code you will write), but by following this rule, it is always clear who owns the data and who can modify it. Since you copy keys and values, the code will work since it simply isn't possible for a user to overwrite the numbers you inserted into the table, even if they are pointers to memory on the caller's stack.

Key and Value Types

Since you cannot generally know how to copy, compare, and free keys and values, you must provide a mechanism for the user to tell you. You also had to do this when generating code, but now you can do so without invoking macros. You define types for keys and values; any user who wants to create a table must provide one for each. The types are just pointers to functions implementing the operations you need:

```
typedef unsigned int (*hash_func)(void const *);
typedef bool (*compare_func)(void const *, void const *);
typedef void (*destructor_func)(void *);
typedef void *(*copy_func)(void const *);

struct key_type {
  hash_func hash;
  compare_func cmp;
  copy_func cpy;
  destructor_func del;
};

struct value_type {
  copy_func cpy;
  destructor_func del;
};
```

You must be able to compute a hash value and compare two keys for keys, and you must be able to copy and free data for both keys and values.

The operations you will implement are as follows:

```
struct hash_table *
new_table(struct key_type const *key_type, struct value_type
const *value_type);
```

CHAPTER 5   ADDING APPLICATION KEYS AND VALUES

```
void
delete_table(struct hash_table *table);

void
add_map(struct hash_table *table, void const *key, void const
*value);
void
delete_key(struct hash_table *table, void const *key);
void *const
lookup_key(struct hash_table *table, void const *key);
```

The const declarations indicate that you won't take ownership of keys and values. (You cannot specify that you won't store them either, but you will make copies to ensure that data doesn't change behind the table's back.)

Hash Map Definition

The hash map you implement is based on the linear probing strategy. It is not that different from what you saw in Chapter 4, but you'll add a cached hash key in the bins, so you don't need to recompute hash values when you resize, and the table will have a pointer to the key_type and value_type function definitions.

```
struct bin {
  int in_probe : 1; // The bin is part of a sequence of
                        used bins
  int is_empty : 1; // The bin does not contain a value (but
                        might still be
                     // in a probe sequence)

  unsigned int hash_key; // cached hash key
  void *key;             // pointer to the actual key
  void *val;             // pointer to the value
};
```

```
struct hash_table {
  struct bin *bins;
  unsigned int size;
  unsigned int used;
  unsigned int active;
  struct key_type const *key_type;
  struct value_type const *value_type;
};
```

The probing strategy is the same one you used before:

```
unsigned int static p(unsigned int k, unsigned int i,
unsigned int m)
{
  return (k + i) & (m - 1);
}
```

Because you have to look up operations in a type structure pointed to by a table, calling operations will be very verbose. So, add some helper functions:

The hash function uses the key type's hash function to map a user key to a hash key.

```
static inline unsigned int
hash(struct hash_table *table, void const *key)
{
  return table->key_type->hash(key);
}
```

The copy_key and copy_val functions use the key and value types to make a copy of input. The free_key and free_val functions, similarly, use the types to free memory.

```c
static inline void *
copy_key(struct hash_table *table, void const *key)
{
  return table->key_type->cpy(key);
}

static inline void *
copy_val(struct hash_table *table, void const *val)
{
  return table->value_type->cpy(val);
}

static inline void
free_key(struct hash_table *table, void *key)
{
  table->key_type->del(key);
}

static inline void
free_val(struct hash_table *table, void *val)
{
  table->value_type->del(val);
}
```

Finally, with a function that doesn't involve the types, is_active_bin checks if a bin is currently active (i.e., it is part of a probe and not marked as empty):

```c
static inline bool
is_active_bin(struct bin *bin)
{
  return bin->in_probe && !bin->is_empty;
}
```

Creating and Resizing a Table

The creation and resizing processes are largely identical to what you have seen in Chapter 4, so I do not explain it in detail again here. You use an init_table() function to initialize tables and update them when resizing. It gets a (new) size and a (possibly empty) sequence of empty bins, and then it updates all the bookkeeping and moves the bins into the new table. The function uses a helper, add_map_internal(), which I get to later when you learn to implement insertion. This function inserts a key to a value map into the table, assuming you already have the hash value and have already copied the key and value data, which will be the case in init_table(), because you can get it from existing bins.

```
// add_map_internal is a helper function for add_map that
// expects us to have already computed the hash_key for the
// key and copied the key and value. It inserts the
// hash_key/key -> value mapping in the table.
static void
add_map_internal(struct hash_table *table,
                 unsigned int hash_key,
                 void *key_copy, void *value_copy);

// Initialize the table with `size` bins, and then copy
// the bins from `begin` to `end` into the table.
static void
init_table(struct hash_table *table, unsigned int size,
           struct bin *begin,
           struct bin *end)
{
  // Initialize table members
  table->bins = malloc(size * sizeof *table->bins);
  table->size = size;
```

```
  table->used = 0;
  table->active = 0;

  // Initialize bins
  struct bin empty_bin = {.in_probe = false,
                          .is_empty = true};
  for (unsigned int i = 0; i < table->size; i++) {
    table->bins[i] = empty_bin;
  }

  // Copy the old bins to the new table
  for (struct bin *bin = begin; bin != end; bin++) {
    if (!bin->is_empty) {
      add_map_internal(table, bin->hash_key,
                       bin->key, bin->val);
    }
  }
}
```

When you create a new table, you initialize it with the initial size (MIN_SIZE in this implementation) and with an empty sequence of existing bins (begin and end arguments are both NULL).

```
#define MIN_SIZE 8

struct hash_table *
new_table(struct key_type const *key_type, struct value_type
const *value_type)
{
  struct hash_table *table = malloc(sizeof *table);
  table->key_type = key_type;
  table->value_type = value_type;
  init_table(table, MIN_SIZE, NULL, NULL);
  return table;
}
```

For resizing, you call `init_table` with the new size and the existing bins. Since `init_table` will overwrite the bins pointer in the table structure, you save a pointer to them in `old_bins_begin` to free them afterward. After a resize, the pointers to keys and values are moved into the new bins by `init_table()` and `add_map_internal()` so you will not leak application memory when you delete the old bins.

```
static void
resize(struct hash_table *table, unsigned int new_size)
{
  // Remember the old bins until we have moved them.
  struct bin *old_bins_begin = table->bins,
             *old_bins_end = old_bins_begin + table->size;

  // Update the table and copy the old active bins to it.
  init_table(table, new_size, old_bins_begin, old_bins_end);

  // finally, free memory for old bins
  free(old_bins_begin);
}
```

Compared to the same hash map in Chapter 4, the main difference is how you move old data into new tables when you resize. Here, you now have to worry about memory management, something you didn't when you only had integer keys and values. This is all taken care of in `init_table()`'s call to `add_map_internal()`, so all you have seen so far is that you get both a key and a hash key from the bins you copy.

Freeing Tables

In the version from Chapter 4, you only needed to free the bins and the table `struct` when you deleted a table, but now you need to free the data you copied into the table as well. The flow is reasonably straightforward; you run through each bin and free any data there. You know if a bin

contains data from the flags set in it, and you can use the is_active_bin()
helper function to check. If there is data there, you need to free the key and
value, which you do using the free_key() and free_val() helpers that
dispatch to the key and value types, respectively.

```
// If there is data in a bin, free it
static inline void
free_bin(struct hash_table *table, struct bin *bin)
{
  if (is_active_bin(bin)) {
    free_key(table, bin->key);
    free_val(table, bin->val);
    bin->is_empty = true; // Delete the bin
    table->active--; // Same bins in use but one less active
  }
}

void
delete_table(struct hash_table *table)
{
  for (struct bin *bin = table->bins; bin != table->bins +
table->size; ++bin) {
    free_bin(table, bin);
  }
  free(table->bins);
  free(table);
}
```

The free_bin() function ignores bins that aren't active, so you can
safely call it with inactive probes. If you are in an active probe, it will free
the data stored in the bin and update the active counter, which you need
for resizing (see Chapter 4).

Lookup

Checking if a key is in the table and returning the value if it is also follows the pattern from Chapter 4. (Spoiler alert: All the operations do.) Checking if a key is in a bin is slightly more complicated now, however, because you store user keys together with hash keys. You need to write a helper function for this:

```
// Check if the bin contains the key. We first check if
// the bin is active, then, if the hash keys match
// (if they don't, we don't need to call a potentially
// expensive key comparison function), and finally,
// we compare the keys.
static inline bool
key_in_bin(struct hash_table *table, struct bin *bin, unsigned
int hash_key,
          void const *key)
{
  return is_active_bin(bin) && bin->hash_key == hash_key &&
        table->key_type->cmp(bin->key, key);
}
```

For a key to be in a bin, the bin must be active (otherwise, a key match would be spurious or match to a deleted key). It must also match the key, as defined by the key type's comparison function. You could check only those two conditions, but you also added a comparison of hash keys. If the key is a match, the hash values will also match, so the comparison doesn't contribute to determining a match. Still, by comparing hash functions first, you can avoid calling the comparison function in the (highly likely) cases where different keys have different hash values.

Next, you need code to find the bin that contains a key. This is a simple matter of following the probe until you find a match or a bin that is not part of a probe, similar to Chapter 4. The probing loop goes in a helper function because you will use it later when inserting and deleting.

```
// Find the bin containing key, or the first bin past the
// end of its probe. It will never return a bin that is in
// a probe and empty, since those cannot contain the key,
// and if we need an empty bin we will search for
// the earliest in the probe using find_empty().
struct bin *
find_key(struct hash_table *table, unsigned int hash_key, void
const *key)
{
  for (unsigned int i = 0; i < table->size; i++) {
    struct bin *bin = table->bins + p(hash_key, i,
table->size);
    if (!bin->in_probe ||
        key_in_bin(table, bin, hash_key, key))
      return bin;
  }
  assert(false); // We should never get here
}
```

The assert(false) statement should never be reached since you can only reach the end of the for loop if you searched the entire table, and resizing prevents this.

There is nothing special about returning the next bin in the probe when you don't find the key. You need to return *something*, and returning the bin after the probe gives you an easy-to-check value. If the return value is not active, it isn't in a probe, so you know you didn't find the key. If the return value is active, you must have found the key. This is all you need to implement the lookup_key() function:

```
void *const
lookup_key(struct hash_table *table, void const *key)
{
```

```
  struct bin *bin = find_key(table, hash(table, key), key);
  return bin->in_probe ? bin->val : NULL;
}
```

This returns a pointer to the value stored in the table, so this is not a copy. Therefore, the return value is void * const. You could also have returned a copy (and the user would then always need to free the return value), but in most uses of hash maps, you want a reference to the value without taking ownership, so that is how the function is implemented.

Adding and Deleting

This section deals with deletion first since that is the simplest. The find_key() function from the previous section is used to locate the bin that contains a given hash key. Then you delete it. (Then you resize it, but there is nothing new to resizing compared to Chapter 4.)

```
void
delete_key(struct hash_table *table, void const *key)
{
  struct bin *bin = find_key(table, hash(table, key), key);
  free_bin(table, bin);

  if (table->active < table->size / 8
      && table->size > MIN_SIZE)
    resize(table, table->size / 2);
}
```

The reason you can call free_bin() on the result of find_key() without checking if you found something is that free_bin() only deletes values in an active bin. If you didn't find key, find_key() would have given you an inactive bin, and then free_bin() would not do anything. So, you only free data if the table contains the key.

The main add_map() function is even simpler:

```
void
add_map(struct hash_table *table,
        void const *key, void const *value)
{
  unsigned int hash_key = hash(table, key);
  void *key_copy = copy_key(table, key);
  void *value_copy = copy_val(table, value);
  add_map_internal(table, hash_key, key_copy, value_copy);
}
```

This simplicity hides the complexity in add_map_internal(). The user-callable add_map() needs to compute the hash key from the user key and copy the key and value, but after that, it can hand over the task to the internal version, which looks like this:

```
static void
add_map_internal(struct hash_table *table,
                 unsigned int hash_key,
                 void *key_copy, void *value_copy)
{
  struct bin *bin = get_bin(table, hash_key, key_copy);
  store_in_bin(table, bin, hash_key, key_copy, value_copy);

  if (table->used > table->size / 2)
    resize(table, table->size * 2);
}
```

(The get_bin() function is defined in the following code. The resizing is still the same as in the previous chapter, so you can ignore that.)

The function first finds the bin that contains the key, or the next free bin in the key's probe, and then it inserts the values in that bin.

The get_bin() function will first try to find a bin that contains the key using the find_key() function. If it finds such a bin, it returns it; otherwise, it will search for the first free bin in the probe.

```
struct bin *
get_bin(struct hash_table *table,
        unsigned int hash_key, void *const key)
{
  struct bin *bin = find_key(table, hash_key, key);
  return bin->in_probe ? bin : find_empty(table, hash_key);
}

// Find the first empty bin in its probe.
struct bin *
find_empty(struct hash_table *table, unsigned int hash_key)
{
  for (unsigned int i = 0; i < table->size; i++) {
    struct bin *bin = table->bins + p(hash_key, i,
    table->size);
    if (bin->is_empty)
      return bin;
  }
  assert(false); // you should never get here
}
```

The only remaining function is store_in_bin(), which is responsible for storing a key/value mapping in a bin. This sounds simple, but the function is perhaps longer than you would expect:

```
static inline void
store_in_bin(struct hash_table *table, struct bin *bin,
unsigned int hash_key,
             void *key, void *value)
```

```
{
    // Update counters based on current state of bin.
    table->active += !!bin->is_empty;
    table->used += !bin->in_probe;

    // Free any key or value currently in the bin.
    free_bin(table, bin);

    // Store the new key and value in the bin.
    *bin = (struct bin){
        .in_probe = true,
        .is_empty = false,
        .hash_key = hash_key,
        .key = key,
        .val = value,
    };
}
```

The complicated bits are the first two lines that keep track of the table's counters. After that, you free any values already in the bin and then update the bin with the new values, which is all pretty straightforward.

The counters in the table, `active` and `used`, are the same as in Chapter 4. You keep track of how many bins are used (i.e. part of a probe) and how many are active (i.e., both part of a probe and not empty). The `in_probe` and `is_empty` flags in the bin tell you all you need to update the counters. If they were always 0 or 1, you could add `is_empty` to `active` and, that way, increment `active` if and only if the bin is empty. Similarly, adding `!in_probe` to `used` would increment `used` only when a bin is not in a probe. The `is_empty` and `in_probe` members are not `bool`, however, but `int : 1`, so you are not guaranteed that their numerical value is 0 or 1, only that "`false`" means 0, while "`true`" could be any non-zero value. You are guaranteed, however, that `!x` will be 1 if `x` is non-zero and 0 otherwise, and you are guaranteed that `!!x` will be 1 if `x` is non-zero and 0 otherwise. That is the explanation behind the weird counting in the function.

Conclusions

Extending the simple hash tables from earlier with user-defined keys and values has little to do with hashing or table strategies and more with general memory management and dealing with C's lack of generics. C doesn't support generics except in the limited case of void pointers, and it doesn't support polymorphism except as function pointers. Those are the tools you have to work with.

This chapter covered two approaches—you can generate code using macros or restrict yourself to pointers and use void * as a generic type. Both approaches have pros and cons, so the right choice will depend on the application for which you need a hash table.

In both cases, you need to deal with *hashing*—getting a hash value from a user key—*comparison*—so you can provide functionality for comparing keys—and *memory management*—both in the sense that you know whether the table or the user has ownership of the data or so you can ensure that you don't leak memory or risk freeing memory more than once.

CHAPTER 6

Heuristic Hash Functions

The main focus of this book is on the practical implementation of hash tables, with hash functions being a secondary but crucial aspect. The book starts with the assumption that the hash keys are uniformly distributed, although this is often not the case in real-world scenarios. In this chapter, I introduce you to commonly used heuristic hash functions, which are invaluable in such situations. The next chapter explores an approach that can provide stronger probabilistic guarantees, enhancing your understanding and application of hash functions. You can download the code at https://github.com/mailund/JoyChapter6.

As you embark on this chapter, you'll begin by considering two cases where your data is not randomly distributed. To help you visualize this, assume you have data that can be represented in 16 bits with 64 data points. You'll map these data points within the length ranges of 8, 16, 32, and 64 for powers of 2 or 7, 17, 31, and 67 for tables with lengths that are prime numbers. This will allow you to understand how keys are distributed over bins with tables of different sizes without worrying about conflict resolution and load at this stage.

I set up two pathological cases, one where I have consecutive numbers from 0 to 128 and one where I have the same numbers but shifted two bits. The latter is to emulate the case where you have pointers that are four bytes apart. Usually, you will have pointers aligned with computer words, which are likely to be four or eight bytes apart, so the lowest two or four bits will be zero. The numbers can all be represented in 8 bits, but I allow the hash keys to take values in 16 bits and mask them down to the lower half of the bits.

I plotted the first case in Figure 6-1 and the second in Figure 6-2. I do not plot the input (application) keys. These are all the numbers from 0 to 128, and you would not be able to see them in either plot except as a thin bar to the left of the histogram. They would be at the very left end of the x-axis since $N = 2^{16} = 65,536$ and 128 is tiny compared to 65,536. Even if you shift them two bits up, you only get to 512, which would still be at the far left of the range. What the plots show are the hash keys when binned to the different table sizes using masking or modulus.

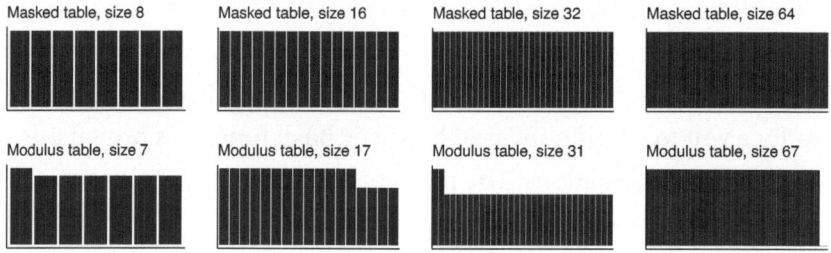

Figure 6-1. *Consecutive numbers directly mapped to hash keys*

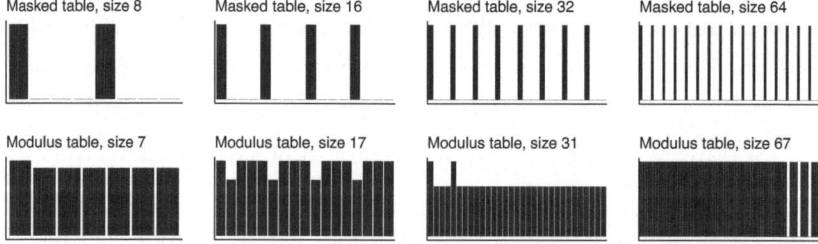

Figure 6-2. *Numbers shifted two bits directly mapped to hash keys*

Although the input keys are far from evenly spread across the range of all possible keys, you, of course, get a relatively even distribution when you bin them by mapping using masking or modulus to the table range. This is somewhat artificial, and an artifact of the way taking the remainder works. As long as you cover the whole range of the smaller table, you will see a good spread there. This is not what I want you to focus on. What is interesting is the difference in behavior when you go from covering the full range of [128] to only mapping every fourth key in [512].

In the first case, you get good spreads for both the masked and the prime-number hash tables, while in the second case, you only get a good spread for the prime-number-sized hash tables. That should not be a surprise. You base your bins on the lower bits when you mask them, and you get a poor distribution when you shift them. The second case is the worst setup for masking. Thus, better hash functions are needed than just masking/taking modulus. One of the reasons people prefer to use hash keys modulo a prime is precisely to avoid this problem. With good hash functions, however, you can get closer to the goal of randomly distributed hash keys when you mask the lowest bits. Heuristics for this is considered in this chapter.

What Makes a Good Hash Function?

Before you see how to engineer these hash functions, consider these properties:

1.   They should be fast to compute.

2.   They should be deterministic.[1]

3.   They should aim at distributing values uniformly in their target domain.

---

[1] When I say deterministic here, I mean that a hash function should always produce the same output on the same input. There are plenty of randomized hash functions in the sense that they use random numbers as part of their construction. You fix these random numbers when you use the function to hash application keys. You can change from one hash function to another by picking new random numbers, but you can't change them at arbitrary times if you want your function to consistently give you the same output for the same input. Universal hashing, which is discussed in the next chapter, uses random numbers to create deterministic hash functions.

You always want fast computation, and obviously also for hash functions. The goal of hash tables is to achieve constant time lookups, but if the hash function is slow at computing the hash key, then much of the efficiency is lost. If time is so vital that you prefer masking bits instead of calculating the remainder modulus a prime, then the hash function shouldn't be slower than the modulus operation. This means that you need bit-wise operations rather than arithmetic operations and adding and subtracting rather than multiplying and dividing.

The second property is essential. If the hash function is not deterministic, you might end up with two different keys for the same value. If the hash key changes each time you want to look up a value, the hash table cannot do lookups. However, this point does not mean that you cannot use randomization. As you will see later, you can use randomization to avoid poor performance of hash functions on pathological data where values map to a small range of hash table bins. If you use random values, however, they need to be parameters to the hash function so you can get deterministic behavior out of it.

The third property is why you need hash functions, and this property is the hardest to achieve. You get the best performance in a hash table when keys are spread uniformly over the hash table bin. If the hash table produces random keys, you will also get a uniform spread in bins. If it does not, there are no runtime guarantees. This is, unfortunately, impossible to guarantee with a single deterministic hash function. If you map k-bit values to a l-bit range, you map 2^k possible values into 2^l keys. The best you can achieve if the map is uniform, is to map 2^{k-1} values to each key. An adversary that knows your hash function can exploit this and maximize the number of collisions you get. You can mitigate this with an ensemble of different hash functions by choosing a hash function dependent on the data. You can avoid adversarial data by randomly selecting (deterministic) hash functions. With a single good hash function that tends to map similar data to very different hash keys, you usually get good performance without randomization tricks.

Hashing Computer Words

The remainder of this chapter considers two cases. First, you have values that you can fit into a single computer word, and you want to scramble up the values to make them evenly distributed. Second, in the more general case, you have a sequence of bytes for each value where the length varies from value to value. Any case that does not fit the first can be handled by the second since you can serialize any data to a stream of bytes, even though it might require some programming to get there for some data structures.

In the following, I only consider the example case where the numbers were shifted two bits to the right. When you use consecutive numbers from 0 to 63 and shift these by two bits, the result still fits into a single byte. Although I use 32-bit words in all the functions, remember that in the input, the only non-zero bits are in the least significant byte. Also, I mask the hash keys to the 16 least significant bits for plotting purposes.

Now, from the identity hash function, the problem you had with the masked tables was that the lower bits were all zeros. Having 3/4 of the bytes in the input values identical makes the test data somewhat adversarial. If you are hashing something like pointers, it is not unusual that the least significant bits are identical. If some bits in the input are always the same, their input domain is effectively smaller, and no hash function can compensate for this when scrambling the input. Still, if the hash function scrambles the remaining bits well, you should still get good performance.

Before addressing the hash functions, you need to understand some terminology. Consider Figure 6-3, which shows the components of a hash function when you deal with an entire computer word as a single unit. You can assume that you have a parameter that goes into the function. This gives you a way to parameterize a function, and this value can be random as long as you use the same parameter every time you hash a value. The

parameter can potentially be used to randomize a function if you get poor
performance.

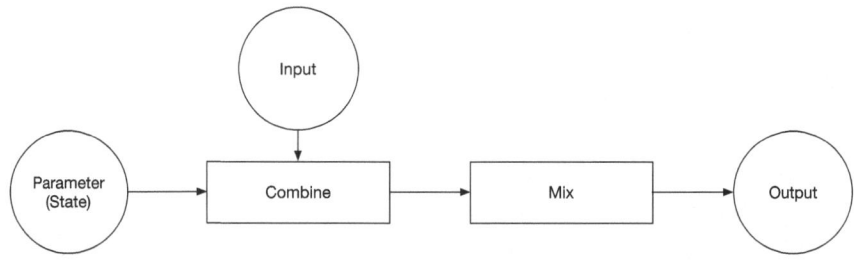

Figure 6-3. *Components of a single-word hash function*

This parameter is also called a *state* (or *initial state*) because it works
as an intermediate state when you hash multiple words; see Figure 6-4.
Multiple words do not necessarily refer to complete computer words here
but also to individual sub-keys, such as the four bytes, which a 32-bit
computer word consists of. When you split a word into individual bytes or
hash over multiple-word values, the output of a single computation in the
hash function behaves as the input of the next, and you call such values the
states of the function as you process the input.

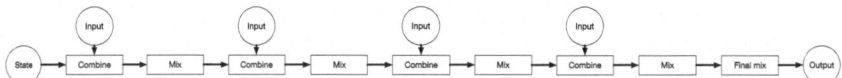

Figure 6-4. *Components of a multiple-word hash function*

When you hash, you first combine the input with the state of the
function, starting from the initial state. Combining means that you XOR or
add the state to the input. Adding the input to the state is a slightly better
choice for scrambling the bits in the input since a single bit in the input
will only affect a single bit in the output with XOR. When you add, a carry
bit can propagate a single input bit several bits to the left in the result. For
maximum speed, on the other hand, XOR is preferable.

You then mix up the result after combining the input and state. In this step, you attempt to modify the state such that each bit in the state will affect several other bits as a result of the mixing. If you hash a value consisting of multiple components—bytes or words—you perform several combine and mix steps, and you might have some additional mixing after you have processed all the input.

Most functions I present in this chapter are taken from Bob Jenkins' excellent web page at http://www.burtleburtle.net/bob/hash/doobs.html, in some cases with minor modifications. I have not included all hash functions described there, but I have selected a few that tend to perform well. If you want to explore more functions, Jenkins' web page is a good starting point. All functions take a 32-bit integer as its state input (even when this value is ignored), a 32-bit bit word for the input, and produce a 32-bit integer as output.

Additive Hashing

One of the simplest hash functions is the *additive hashing* function.[2] This function, shown here, combines the input and the state by addition and without mixing. It does move all the four bits in a 32-bit word to the least significant byte, so the lower bits are potentially affected by the full 32-bit input. The higher bits do not affect the lower bits if you simply add hash and input in the function. For the test input, where the three most significant bytes are all zeros, it behaves exactly as the identity function when the state parameter is 0; see Figure 6-5. When state is not 0, it still leaves the two lowest bits constant on the input. The two lowest bits will

---

[2] The simplest I have seen was used to hash ASCII strings and only used the first character. For standard ASCII, there are only 128 characters (they use seven bits per character), while for Extended ASCII there are 256. That is not the bad part, however. If you hash common words, such as variable names in a program, then these do not use the full set of ASCII characters. Using only the first character of a string is a very poor hash function.

be copied directly from the state parameter and will not be affected by the input.

```
uint32_t additive_hash(uint32_t state, uint32_t input)
{
    uint32_t hash = state;
    uint8_t *p = (uint8_t*)&input;

    // combine
    hash += *(p++);
    hash += *(p++);
    hash += *(p++);
    hash += *p;

    return hash;
}
```

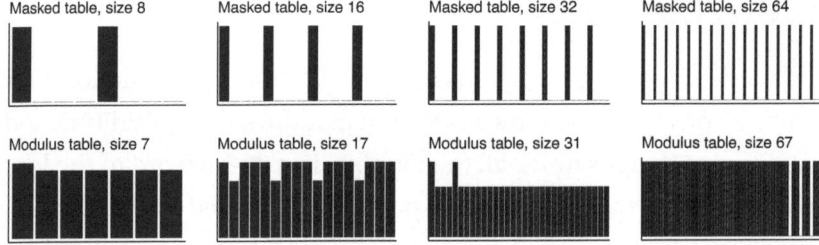

Figure 6-5. *Additive hashing*

Since the sizes of your masked hash tables are 8, 16, 32, and 64, the binned keys are 3, 4, 5, and 6 bits. The additive hashing function can only modify 1, 2, 3, and 4, respectively, since the lower two bits are constant. The input spans all possible bit-patterns of these, so you already have the best possible spread you can get using this hash function, regardless of the state parameter. It cannot perform better than the identity hash function on the test data.

Rotating Hashing

On many hardware architectures that have a rotate operation, implemented using shift and OR, you can write a high-speed hash function that operates using rotate and XOR.

```
#define rot(x,k) (((x)<<(k)) | ((x)>>(32-(k))))
uint32_t rotating_hash(uint32_t state, uint32_t input)
{
    uint32_t hash = state;
    uint8_t *p = (uint8_t*)&input;

    //      mix            ; combine
    hash ^=                  *(p++);
    hash += rot(hash, 4) ^ *(p++);
    hash += rot(hash, 4) ^ *(p++);
    hash += rot(hash, 4) ^ *p;

    return hash;
}
```

Big-endian and small-endian architectures will combine the input bytes in different order. To reverse the order in which you add the bytes, you can implement the function like this:

```
uint32_t rotating_hash(uint32_t state, uint32_t input)
{
    uint32_t hash = state;
    uint8_t *p = ((uint8_t*)&input) + 3;

    //      mix            ; combine
    hash ^=                  *(p--);
    hash += rot(hash, 4) ^ *(p--);
    hash += rot(hash, 4) ^ *(p--);
```

```
    hash += rot(hash, 4) ^ *p;

    return hash;
}
```

This function rotates the hash function state in each mixing step and combines one byte at a time using XOR. Rotating can preserve input bits through many cycles of input, but for a single computer word, it does not work well in this application. If you first combine with the byte that contains different data, as you would do on a big-endian computer, the mixing operations shift out of the lower bits entirely, and the function would only depend on the addition that preserves bit-positions through the three operations; see Figure 6-6. I highlighted the input bytes using boxes; the boxes on the right eight bits show where the input bytes enter the function. With the three first bytes set to 0, as in the test data, and the two least-significant bits at zero as well, you will not get a better spread over bins than you get with additive hashing, although the hash keys are spread out more than with additive hashing. See Figure 6-7.

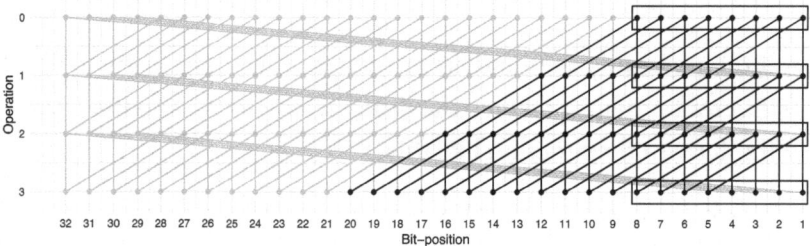

Figure 6-6. *Bits affected by the first input byte (shown in black). Addition (vertical edges) is shown as if it only affects single bits. In actuality, some bits to the left of an addition will be affected*

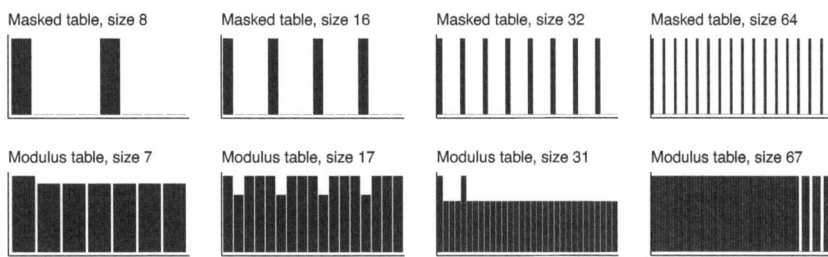

Figure 6-7. *Rotate hashing with the last byte carrying information*

With more bytes in the input, the first byte will wrap around and start affecting later bytes, but the periodicity in when the first byte affects the least significant bytes will be an issue. The best you can hope for is to return the initial byte to the lowest bits minus two, where your 64 keys will take all possible values for your mapped bits. However, this solution only applies to this test data and does not generalize.

When the informative byte in the test data is added in the last combination step, the rotation hash function is a simple XOR between a rotation of the initial state and the variable byte. If the initial state is 0, you will get the same performance as with the additive hashing; see Figure 6-8. Changing the initial state will affect the keys because of the XOR operation, but as with additive hashing, no choice of initial state will allow you to have anything but a constant for the last two bits in the key when the last two bits are constant in the input.

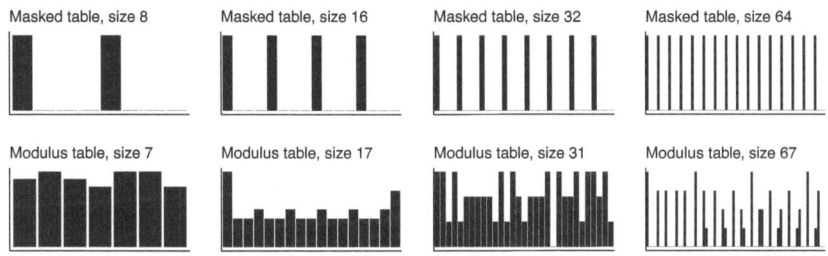

Figure 6-8. *Rotate hashing with the first byte carrying information*

Another way to plot the performance of the hash function is to show how the input bit-patterns translate to output bit-patterns. For the rotating hash function, I have done this in Figures 6-9 and 6-10. The performance of the masking hash tables can be seen by looking at the last 3, 4, 5, and 6 bits. Here, you see that the two least significant bits do not change for the example input, so you get poor performance.

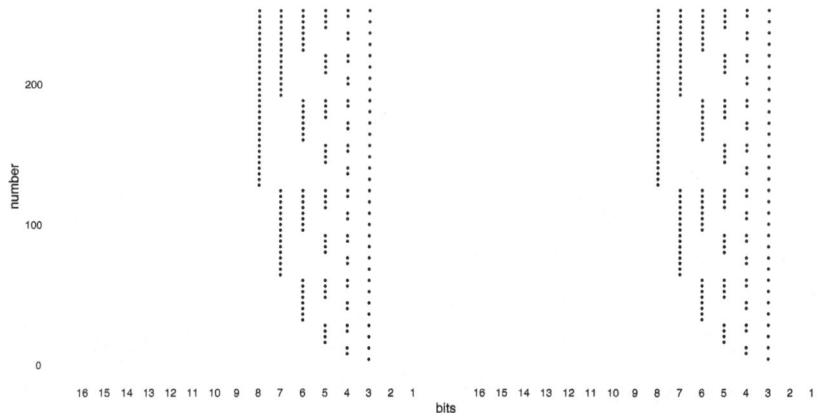

Figure 6-9. *Input and output bit-patterns for the rotating hash function when the input is least-significant-byte last*

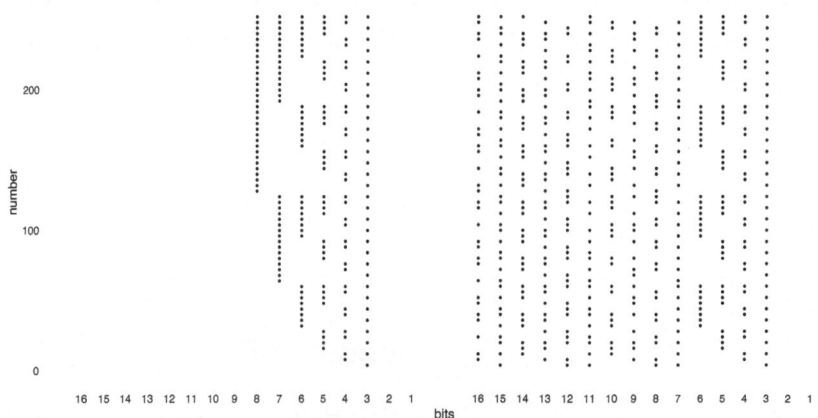

Figure 6-10. *Input and output bit-patterns for the rotating hash function when the input is least-significant-byte first*

One-at-a-Time Hashing

The one-at-a-time hash function, developed by Bob Jenkins, uses addition to combine the state and the input, one byte at a time. It then mixes the result using bit-wise shift, addition, and XOR. You can implement it in two different ways, varying in the order in which you add the bytes in the input. Either this:

```
uint32_t one_at_a_time_hash(uint32_t state, uint32_t input)
{
    uint32_t hash = state;
    uint8_t *p = (uint8_t*)&input;

    // combine    ; mix
    hash += *(p++); hash += (hash << 10); hash ^= (hash >> 6);
    hash += *(p++); hash += (hash << 10); hash ^= (hash >> 6);
    hash += *(p++); hash += (hash << 10); hash ^= (hash >> 6);
    hash += *p;     hash += (hash << 10); hash ^= (hash >> 6);

    // final mix
    hash += (hash << 3);
    hash ^= (hash >> 11);
    hash += (hash << 15);

    return hash;
}
```

Or this:

```
uint32_t one_at_a_time_hash(uint32_t state, uint32_t input)
{
    uint32_t hash = state;
    uint8_t *p = ((uint8_t*)&input) + 3;

    // combine    ; mix
```

```
hash += *(p--); hash += (hash << 10); hash ^= (hash >> 6);
hash += *(p--); hash += (hash << 10); hash ^= (hash >> 6);
hash += *(p--); hash += (hash << 10); hash ^= (hash >> 6);
hash += *p;     hash += (hash << 10); hash ^= (hash >> 6);

// final mix
hash += (hash << 3);
hash ^= (hash >> 11);
hash += (hash << 15);

return hash;
}
```

Assuming you can assign and perform an operation in one instruction, so += and ^= are one operation, you spend seven operations on combining, 4 × 6 on mixing and six operations on the final mix, for a total of 30 operations.

Similar to how the rotating hash was visualized, you can show how the one-at-a-time hash function moves bits around. In Figure 6-11, I show how the bits in the first byte propagate down through the operations, and in Figure 6-12, I show how the bits in the last byte propagate. Each mixing step consists of two operations, so the input bytes are added as operations 0, 2, 4, and 6. The last three operations are the final mixing.

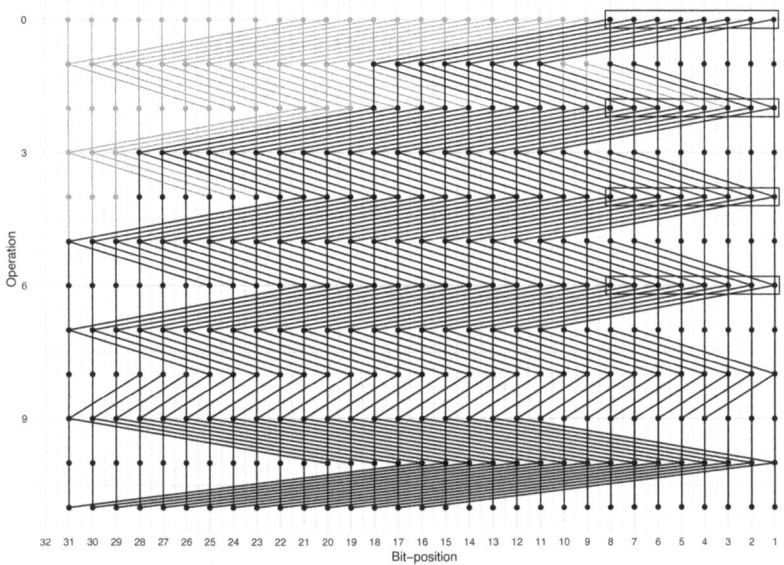

Figure 6-11. *Bits affected by the first input byte (shown in black) using one-at-a-time hashing*

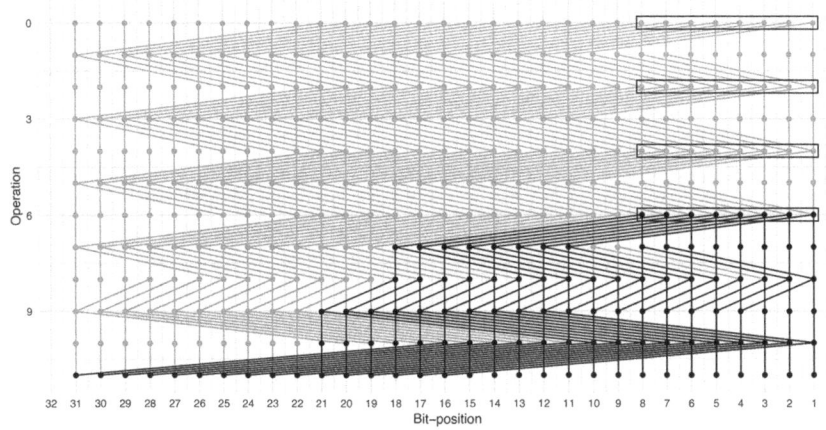

Figure 6-12. *Bits affected by the first last byte (shown in black) using one-at-a-time hashing*

Plotting how input bits propagate to the output bits tells you how many output bits are affected by your input and, more importantly, how many input bits each output bit depends on. I plotted this dependency for the least- and the second-least significant bit—the bits that were constant in your previous attempts at hash functions—in Figures 6-13 and 6-14. This isn't the entire story since some of the operations can cancel each other, but you can see that the least significant bit depends on all the input bits from the first byte and all except bit 3 for the last byte. For the second-least significant bit, you can see that it depends on all the bits in the first byte and four out of eight of the last byte.

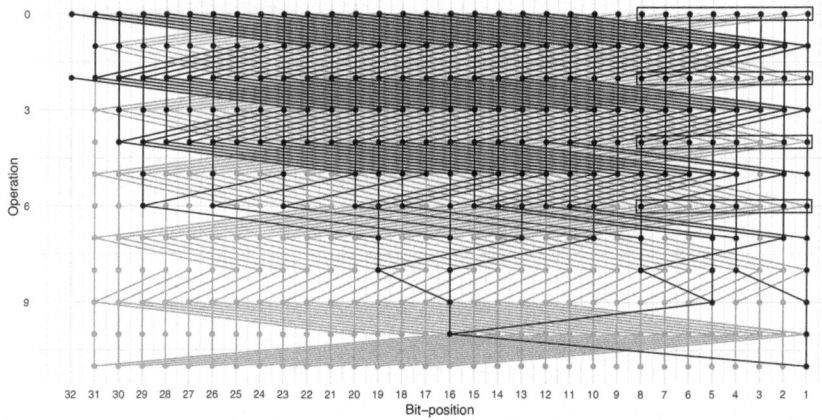

Figure 6-13. *Dependencies for the least significant bit in one-at-a-time hashing*

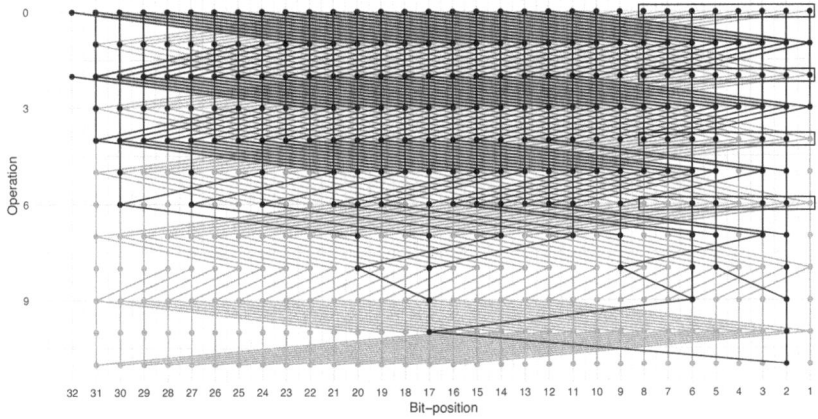

Figure 6-14. *Dependencies for the second-least significant bit in one-at-a-time hashing*

Based on these observations, you expect that this hash function performs better on your test data, which seems to be the case. See Figures 6-15 and 6-16. Since the output bits depend on all the bits in the first byte and only some of the bits in the last byte, you might expect that putting the informative byte in your test data as the first byte would be slightly better, but both options seem to work well.

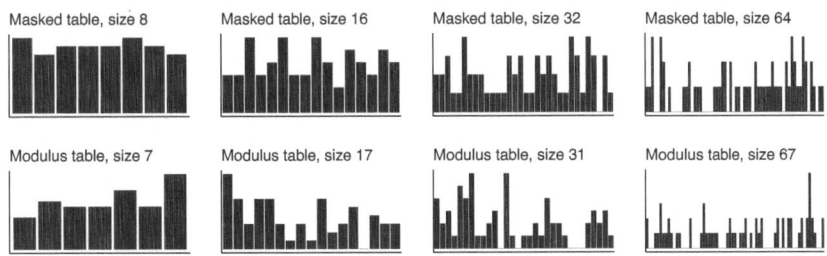

Figure 6-15. *One-at-a-time hashing adding the informative byte in the first combine operation*

167

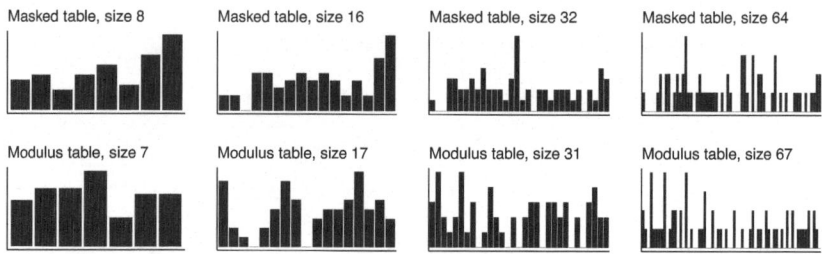

Figure 6-16. *One-at-a-time hashing adding the informative byte in the last combine operation*

You can also see that the output bits depend on combinations of the initial state and the input, suggesting that poor performance on adversarial data can be improved by changing the initial state.

The bit-patterns for the input and output of this hash function are shown in Figures 6-17 and 6-18. You can see that you propagate some of the variation in the input to the least-significant bits.

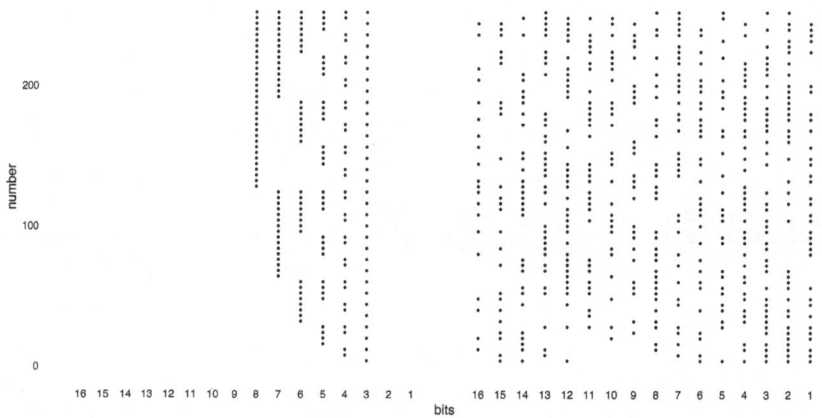

Figure 6-17. *Input and output bit-patterns for the one-at-a-time hash function when the input is least-significant-byte first*

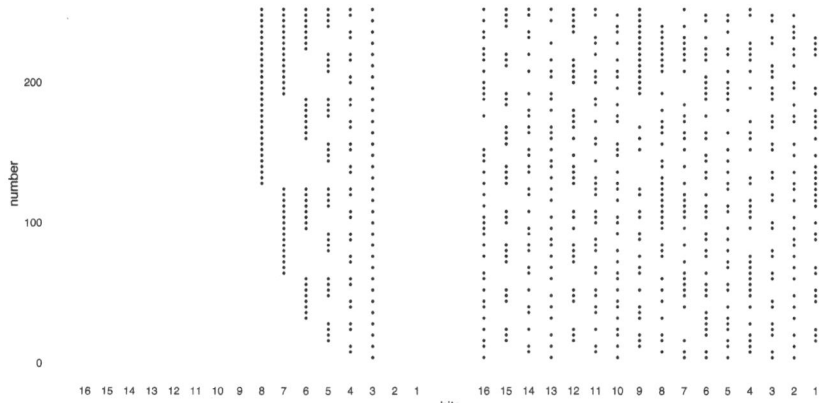

Figure 6-18. *Input and output bit-patterns for the one-at-a-time hash function when the input is least-significant-byte last*

The initial state affects the hash keys when you use rotating hashing, but it will not change the two least significant bits, which are constant on the example input. For one-at-a-time hashing, these bits *do* vary with the initial state. See Figures 6-19 to 6-22. This should give you some hope that, if the hash function performs poorly on specific data, you can change the initial state and get better performance.

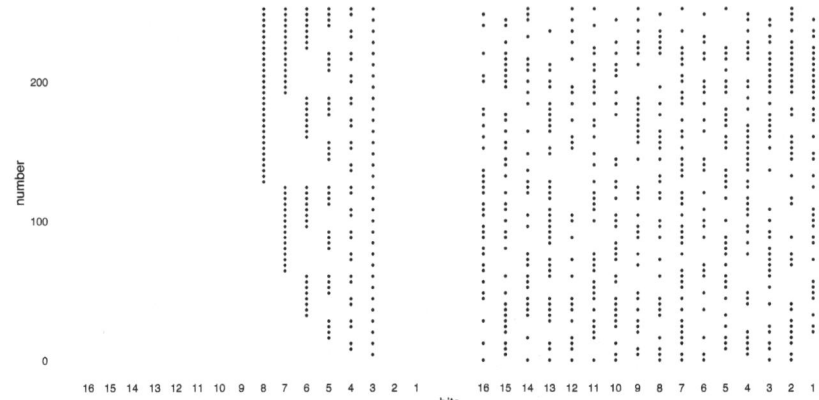

Figure 6-19. *Input and output bit-patterns for the one-at-a-time hash function when the input is least-significant-byte first and initial state set to 1*

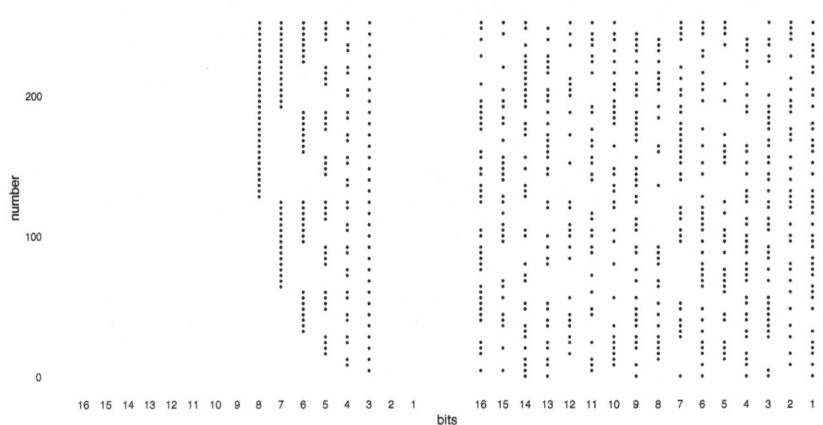

Figure 6-20. *Input and output bit-patterns for the one-at-a-time hash function when the input is least-significant-byte first and initial state set to 0x9e3779b9*

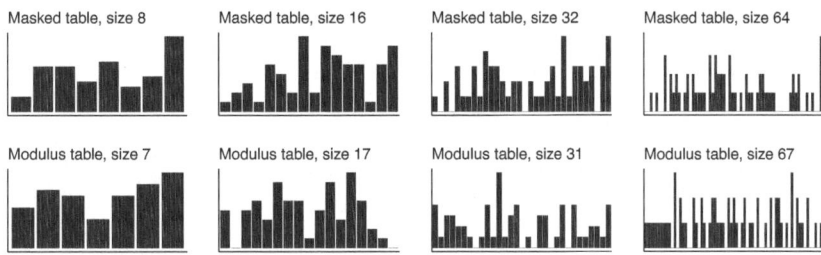

Figure 6-21. *One-at-a-time hashing adding the informative byte in the last combine operation and the initial state set to 1*

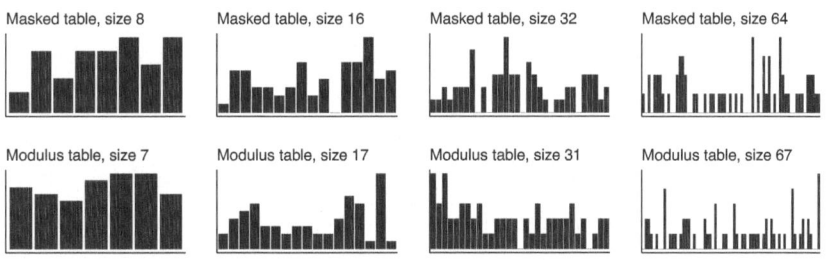

Figure 6-22. *One-at-a-time hashing adding the informative byte in the last combine operation and the initial state set to 0x9e3779b9*

Jenkins Hashing

The Jenkins' `loopup2` function operates on full computer words and looks as follows:

```
uint32_t jenkins_hash(uint32_t state, uint32_t input)
{
    uint32_t a, b; a = b = 0x9e3779b9;
    uint32_t c = state;

    // combine
    a += input;
```

```
// mix
a -= b; a -= c; a ^= (c>>13);
b -= c; b -= a; b ^= (a<<8);
c -= a; c -= b; c ^= (b>>13);
a -= b; a -= c; a ^= (c>>12);
b -= c; b -= a; b ^= (a<<16);
c -= a; c -= b; c ^= (b>>5);
a -= b; a -= c; a ^= (c>>3);
b -= c; b -= a; b ^= (a<<10);
c -= a; c -= b; c ^= (b>>15);

return c;
}
```

This hash function uses more operations than one-at-a-time. It uses one operation for combining and 9×4 on mixing, so a total of 37. For larger keys, however, you can operate on data in chunks of 12 bytes, where you can combine 12 bytes in three operations and still mix in 36 operations to get a performance of $36/12n = 3n$ operations for keys of n bytes. The one-at-a-time function will use $2n - 1$ operations for combining, $20n$ for mixing, and six for the final mix, with a total of $40n + 5$ operations. You'll learn about hashing variable length keys later in this chapter.

In this implementation, I set the variable c to the initial state, but in reality, all three variables, a, b, and c, should be considered the state of the function. When you hash more than a single word, all three variables move the state from one word to the next.

A plot of how individual bits move through this function's mixing step gets complicated and does not provide much insight into the function. You can, however, plot the input and output bit-patterns (see Figures 6-23 and 6-24) and the corresponding hash table performance (see Figures 6-25 and 6-26).

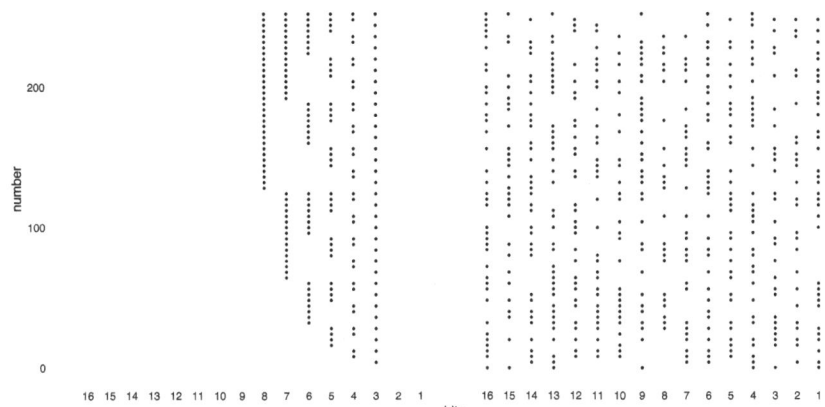

Figure 6-23. *Input and output bit-patterns for Jenkins' lookup2 hash function when the initial state is set to 0*

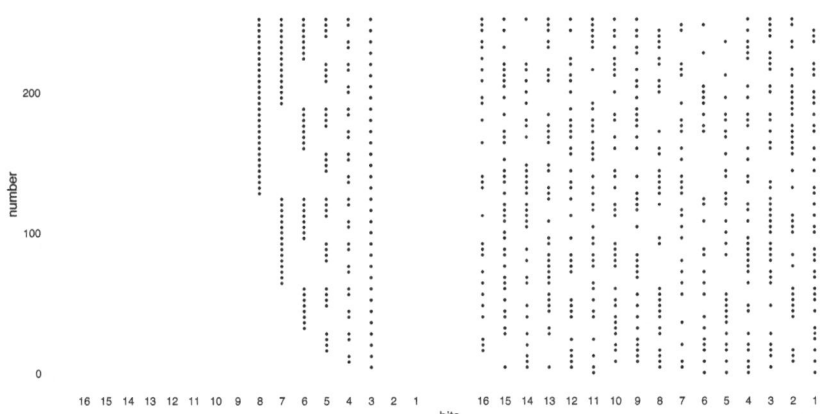

Figure 6-24. *Input and output bit-patterns for Jenkins' lookup2 hash function when the initial state is set to 0x9e3779b9*

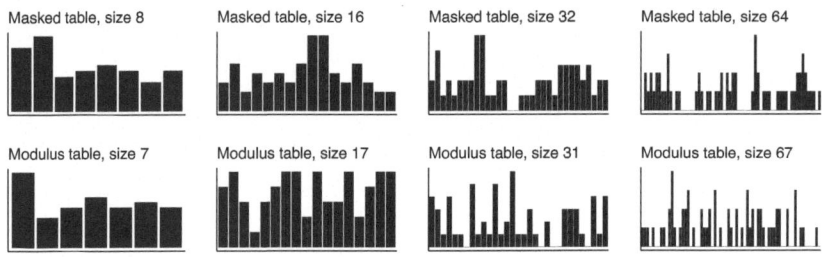

Figure 6-25. *Jenkins' lookup2 hashing with initial state 0*

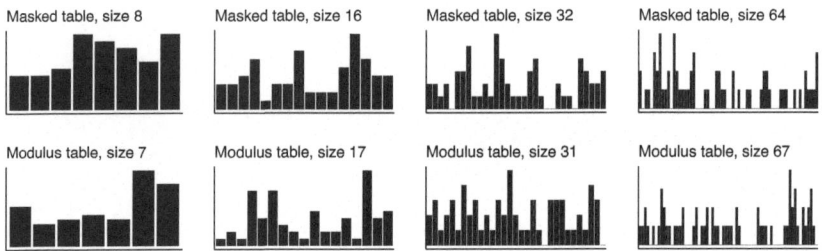

Figure 6-26. *Jenkins' lookup2 hashing with initial state 0x9e3779b9*

Figures 6-25 and 6-26 show the performance of this function on the test data for two different initial states. You get a good spread for either initial state, and the difference between using one state and another is apparent.

A successor, lookup3, is more complex but also faster on larger input data than what is considered here. It is a good choice for hashing entire files. For a hash table, however, lookup2 is a good choice and more straightforward to implement.

In Figure 6-27, I plotted the performance of the different hash functions as I implemented them. I normalized the time measures so they are relative to the mean of the identity function. As expected, the complex functions are slower than the simplest functions, with the Jenkins function about a factor of ten slower than the identity.

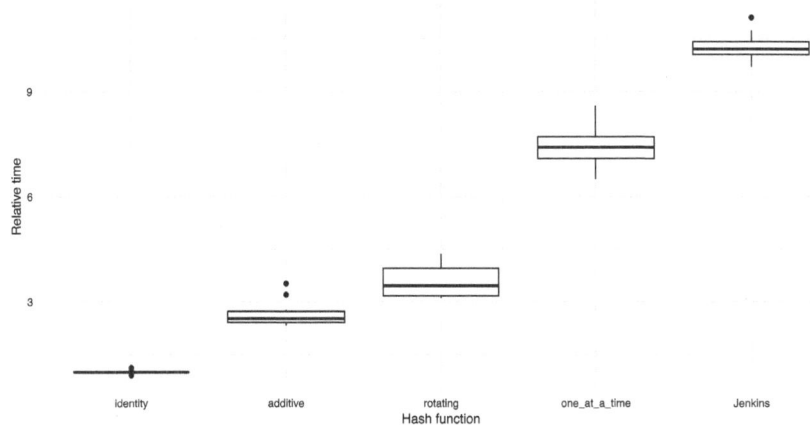

Figure 6-27. *Hash function speed (normalized by the mean performance of the identity function)*

Hashing Strings of Bytes

There is not much difference between hashing a single computer word and a string of bytes of variable length except for a loop. You do not have to worry about the endianness of byte keys since byte keys come in the same order on all software. You can, of course, iterate through the bytes in any order, but there is less reason to worry about it since you can assume that all bytes in such keys would carry information.

I include the length of the key in the signature of hash functions on byte keys. For C strings, you could exploit that these are null-terminated, but this will only work when the keys *are* strings. It will not work if you serialize a general data structure and then hash it. For the Jenkins hash function, you also need to know the length of the input to handle the input 12 bytes at a time.

The first three functions— additive_hash, rotating_hash, and one_at_a_time_hash–are easy to translate into versions that iterate over a sequence of bytes:

```c
uint32_t additive_hash(uint32_t state, char *input, int len)
{
    uint32_t hash = state;
    for (int i = 0; i < len; i++) {
        // combine
        hash += input[i];
    }
    return hash;
}

#define rot(x,k) (((x)<<(k)) | ((x)>>(32-(k))))
uint32_t rotating_hash(uint32_t state, char *input, int len)
{
    uint32_t hash = state;
    for (int i = 0; i < len; i++) {
        //      mix           combine
        hash += rot(hash, 4) ^ input[i];
    }
    return hash;
}

uint32_t one_at_a_time_hash(uint32_t state, char *input,
int len)
{
    uint32_t hash = state;
    for (int i = 0; i < len; i++) {
        // combine
        hash += input[i];
        // mix
```

```
        hash += (hash << 10); hash ^= (hash >> 6);
    }

    // final mix
    hash += (hash << 3);
    hash ^= (hash >> 11);
    hash += (hash << 15);

    return hash;
}
```

The jenkins_hash function takes a little more work since it handles 12 bytes at a time. It reads these into the three state variables, a, b, and c when there are 12 bytes left, and when there are fewer than 12 bytes, it reads in as many as it can using a switch statement:

```
#define mix(a,b,c)                  \
{                                   \
    a -= b; a -= c; a ^= (c>>13); \
    b -= c; b -= a; b ^= (a<<8);  \
    c -= a; c -= b; c ^= (b>>13); \
    a -= b; a -= c; a ^= (c>>12); \
    b -= c; b -= a; b ^= (a<<16); \
    c -= a; c -= b; c ^= (b>>5);  \
    a -= b; a -= c; a ^= (c>>3);  \
    b -= c; b -= a; b ^= (a<<10); \
    c -= a; c -= b; c ^= (b>>15); \
}
uint32_t jenkins_hash(uint32_t state, char *input, int len)
{
    uint32_t a, b; a = b = 0x9e3779b9;
    uint32_t c = state;
    int k = 0;
```

```
// handle most of the key
while (len >= 12)
{
    a += *((uint32_t*)input);
    b += *((uint32_t*)input + 4);
    c += *((uint32_t*)input + 8);
    mix(a,b,c);
    input += 12;
    len -= 12;
}

// handle the last 11 bytes
c += len;
switch(len) // all the case statements fall through
{
    case 11: c += input[10] << 24;
    case 10: c += input[9]  << 16;
    case 9 : c += input[8]  << 8;
    case 8 : b += input[7]  << 24;
    case 7 : b += input[6]  << 16;
    case 6 : b += input[5]  << 8;
    case 5 : b += input[4];
    case 4 : a += input[3]  << 24;
    case 3 : a += input[2]  << 16;
    case 2 : a += input[1]  << 8;
    case 1 : a += input[0];
        // case 0: nothing left to add
}
mix(a,b,c);

return c;
}
```

In Figures 6-28 through 6-31, I plotted the result of the four hash functions where I hashed each word in the poem *The Walrus and the Carpenter*.[3] All functions work well on these words.

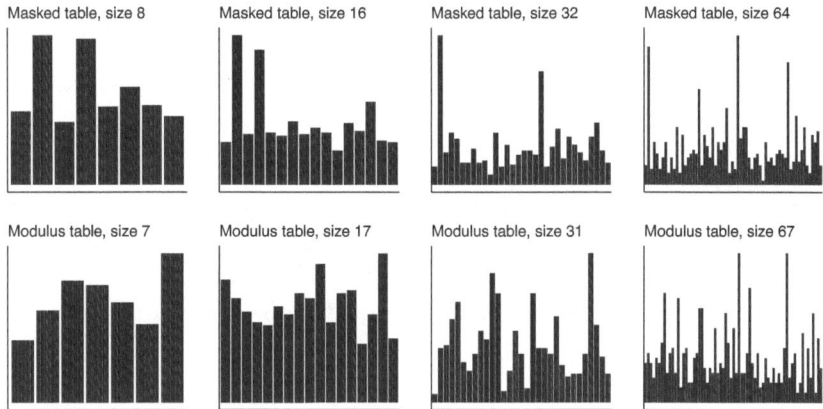

Figure 6-28. *Hashing words using additive hashing*

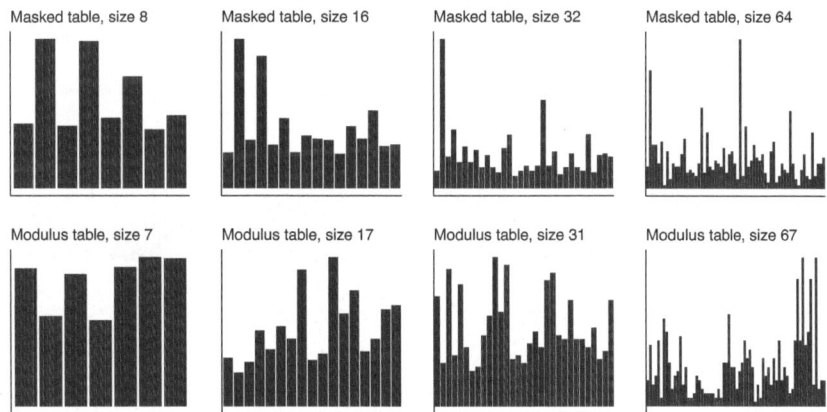

Figure 6-29. *Hashing words using rotating hashing*

---

[3] Taken from https://www.poetryfoundation.org/poems/43914/the-walrus-and-the-carpenter-56d222cbc80a9.

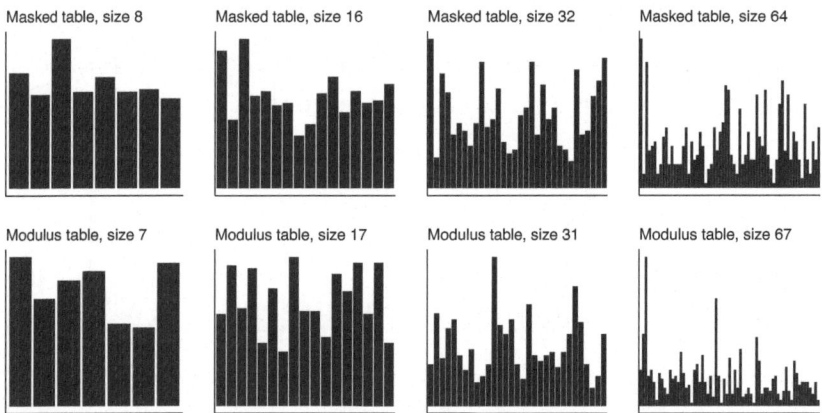

Figure 6-30. *Hashing words using one-at-a-time hashing*

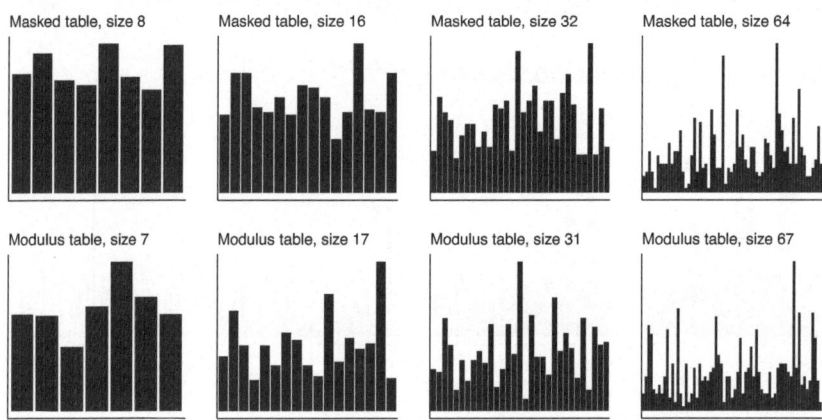

Figure 6-31. *Hashing words using Jenkins hashing*

The functions you have seen in this chapter are fast to evaluate and widely used, but they do guarantee that hash keys are evenly distributed. In general, any fixed hash function, h, cannot guarantee that it maps all keys uniformly over the range $[m]$ for all sets of keys. After all, if keys are taken from N possible values and put into m bins, then h must map N/m keys to at least one bin. If an adversary knew which hash function you are using and could pick the keys to give you the worst performance, they could choose the keys such that you get the most collisions possible.

Randomized algorithms avoid adversarial scenarios by adding stochasticity into the analysis. For hashing, you can pick random functions h. The adversary might know from which family of functions you sample h, but not which function you will use. You do not use worst-case running time in the analysis of these algorithms; the worst case would be the same as if the adversary knew your hash function. Instead, consider the expected running time, over the distribution of functions.

Rehashing the functions you have seen so far does not give you sufficient guarantees to use them in a randomized algorithm analysis. You do not know how different two random choices of a function will be when you choose different function parameters. Universal families of hash functions *do* give you guarantees. That is the topic of Chapter 7.

CHAPTER 7

Universal Hashing

Generally, you cannot assume that an application can produce uniformly distributed keys, and the hash functions in Chapter 6 are only heuristics. They make no guarantees about the results of hashing application keys and thus risk pathological cases where operations are linear rather than constant. You can download this chapter's code at https://github.com/mailund/JoyChapter7.

Since you cannot make assumptions about the hash keys, there is another technique you can employ: randomize the hash *functions*. Instead of using a fixed hash function that might be sensitive to pathological keys, you can use a family of functions and sample from this. You rely on random functions to provide expected constant-time operations. The family of functions needs to satisfy specific properties to provide you with this. You need them to be so-called *universal*, and it is conditional on them being universal that you get guarantees for the expected running times. Of course, expected running times are not worst-case running times; you only see the expected performance on average. You can still risk pathological cases. If that happens, however, you can sample new functions. If you resample functions sufficiently often, you will see the average performance over a long run of table operations.

Because universal hashing is heavily based on probability theory, this chapter is more mathematical than the previous chapters. It is mainly concerned with how to construct hash function families to implement universal hashing, not with proving the probabilistic expectations results.

As before, n refers to the number of keys inserted into a table, m is the size of the table, and $\alpha = n/m$ is the load of the table. I use $x_1, ..., x_n$ to denote keys from the application universe and $y_1, ..., y_n$ to denote hash keys in the range $[m]$. I use $\mathbf{1}$ as the indicator function (i.e., $\mathbf{1}_{event}$ is 1 when the event occurs and 0 when the event does not occur).

Uniformly Distributed Keys

To motivate universal hashing, you must first revisit random keys. Consider chained hashing in a case with load $\alpha < 1$, and consider N operations on the table. Let O_i be the operation number i, $h(x_i) = y_i$ the keys involved in operation O_i, S_i the set of keys in the table after operation $i - 1$, and $T(O_i)$ the time it takes to perform operation O_i.

If the hash keys $y_1, ..., y_n$ are independent and uniformly distributed, you can show that the expected time for each operation is amortized constant time. Consider the expected running time of the N operations.

$$\mathbf{E}\left[\sum_{i=1}^{N} T(O_i)\right]$$

By linearity of expectation, you have

$$\mathbf{E}\left[\sum_{i=1}^{N} T(O_i)\right] = \sum_{i=1}^{N} \mathbf{E}\left[T(O_i)\right]$$

Since the cost of O_i is the number of keys in the bin y_i maps to, you get the following:

$$\mathbf{E}\big[T(O_i)\big]=1+\mathbf{E}\big[\#\{y\in S_i\,|\,y=y_i\}\big]$$

$$=1+\mathbf{E}\left[\sum_{y\in S_i}\mathbf{1}(y=y_i)\right]$$

$$=1+\sum_{y\in S_i}\mathbf{E}\big[\mathbf{1}(y=y_i)\big]$$

$$\leq 1+1+\sum_{y\in S_i,\,y\neq y_i}\Pr\big(\mathbf{1}_{y=y_i}\big)$$

$$\leq 1+1+m\cdot\frac{1}{m}=3$$

In the last step, you use that $|S_i|$ must be less than m when the load is less than 1 and that the keys are uniform so $\Pr(y_i = y_j) = 1/m$ for $y_i \neq y_j$.

Universal Hashing

You cannot assume that keys are random, as they depend on the application. Instead, you can sample random hash functions from a family of functions H. In the previous proof, the keys didn't have to be independent and uniformly distributed; you only needed $\Pr(y_i = y_j) = 1/m$.

You can say that a family of hash functions H is *universal* if

$$\Pr\big(h(x_i)=h(x_j)\big)\leq\frac{1}{m}$$

when $x_i \neq x_j$ and h is chosen at random from H. Notice that it is h that is random here; you make no assumptions about the keys x_i and x_j, other than they are different. (If they were the same, one should hope that the collision probability would be 1, or you have a very poor hash function indeed.)

To get amortized constant time operations in a chained hash table with a load less than 1, you only need the family of hash functions to be universal. You do not need the hash function to map application keys to uniformly distributed hash keys. Universality is also sufficient to show that the expected amortized time for each operation is n/m when the load is larger than 1.

A family of hash functions H is *nearly universal* if

$$\Pr\left(h\left(x_i\right) = h\left(x_j\right)\right) \leq \frac{k}{m}$$

for some constant k when $x_i \neq x_j$ and h is chosen at random from H.

You can repeat the previous proof with nearly universal hash functions and still get constant time operations. The cost will be bounded by $2 + k$ instead of by 3.

Stronger Universal Families

A universal family of hash functions does not give you uniformly distributed hash keys. If you have a family of hash functions that would genuinely give you random hash keys, then for any n application keys $x_1, ..., x_n$ and hash keys $y_1, ..., y_n$ (which could be selected before you sample the hash function, h) you would have the following:

$$\Pr\left(h\left(x_1\right) = y_1, ..., h\left(x_n\right) = y_n\right) = \frac{1}{m} \cdot \frac{1}{m} \cdot ... \cdot \frac{1}{m} = 1/m^n$$

That this should hold for *any* number of keys n is a very strong property of the family of functions, especially considering that you have to create H and be able to sample from it. In general, you cannot sample functions entirely at random. However, you can create and sample from function families with weaker properties that are still stronger than universal families.

A family of hash functions is *k-independent* if for any *k* fixed application and hash keys, $x_1, ..., x_k$ and $y_1, ..., y_k$

$$\Pr\left(h(x_1)=y_1,...,h(x_k)=y_k\right)=1/m^k$$

Families that are two-independent are also called *pairwise-independent* or *strong universal*. Pairwise independent families are also universal, but universal families are not necessarily pairwise independent. Any *k*-independent family is also k'-independent for $k' < k$.

Binning Hash Keys

As you saw earlier, when you map from application keys to hash keys, it is convenient to first map the keys to a large set, [*N*], and then bin these in *m* < *N* bins (i.e., map the hash keys from the large range down to the smaller range).

If you can create a family that is *k*-independent on the larger range, you also need it to be *k*-independent on the smaller range. This property is not true for universal functions, but it is for strong universal families if *m* divides *N*.[1] For example, if *N* is a power of two and the range [*m*] is picked from the lower bits of keys in the range [*m*] then *k*-independent families remain *k*-independent families (i.e. if $N = 2^L$ and $m = 2^{L'}$, $L' < L$ and *h* is a *k*-independent family on [*N*], then $h'(x) = h(x) \mod m$ is a *k*-independent family on [*m*]).

---

[1] If *m* does not divide *N* you cannot make universal families. You simply cannot get the same number of keys mapped to each bin. If *N* is much larger than , however, you get sufficiently close that it doesn't matter in practice.

For $x_1, ..., x_n$ distinct application keys there are $n(n-1)/2$ pairs of keys. A *collision* occurs when $h(x_i) = h(x_j)$ for $i \neq j$. Let X be the number of collisions. The expected number of collisions is then:

$$E[X] = E\left[\sum_{i \neq j} 1_{h(x_i) = h(x_j)} \right]$$

$$= \sum_{i \neq j} \Pr\left(h(x_i) = h(x_j) \right)$$

$$= \frac{n(n-1)}{2} \Pr\left(h(x_i) = h(x_j) \right)$$

$$= \frac{n(n-1)}{2m}.$$

This immediately gives you that if $m \in O(n)$ then $E[X] \in O(n)$. It also gives you that if $m = n^2$ then $E[X] = 1/2 - 1/2n < 1/2$, (i.e., the expected number of collisions is less than one half). Furthermore, since the probability of no collisions is $\Pr(X = 0) = 1 - \Pr(X > 0)$ and

$$\Pr(X > 0) = \sum_{x > 1} \Pr(X = x) < \sum_{x > 1} x \cdot \Pr(X = x) = E[X] < \frac{1}{2}$$

This means that the probability of more than one collision is less than one half, so the probability of no collisions is more than one half. If you pick hash functions at random, and you have a collusion, you expect to get a function that gives you no collisions on a second sample.

Requiring that $m \in O(n^2)$, however, means that you must spend time $O(n^2)$ to initialize and resize tables. That is a high price to pay unless you expect to do more than $O(n^2)$ operations on a table (while still bounding the number of keys that are in the table to $O(n)$).

Expecting zero collisions with high probability is a strong requirement. If you allow collisions and resolve them using the strategies you saw in Chapter 3, you can still get expected constant time operation, although you must make assumptions about k-independence for open addressing.

Collision Resolution Strategies

Using chained hashing, a nearly universal family will give you expected constant time operations, as you saw previously. You cannot guarantee this with open addressing unless you make stronger assumptions about the family of functions.

With *double hashing*, $h(x) = h_1(x) + i \cdot h_2(x)$, you get constant time operations if both functions are drawn from two-independent families.[2]

For linear probing, a five-independent family is needed for expected constant time operations;[3] with five-wise independence the expected probe length is $O((1 - \alpha)^{-5/2})$. For k-independence, $k < 5$, there exist function families that result in logarithmic length probe sequences.[4] In general, the expected number of operations to query a table or construct a table with n elements, as a function of k are these:

Independence	2	3	4	5
Query	$\Theta\left(\sqrt{n}\right)$	$\Theta(\log n)$	$\Theta(\log n)$	$\Theta(1)$
Construction	$\Theta(n \log n)$	$\Theta(n \log n)$	$\Theta(n)$	$\Theta(n)$

The results that require five-independence for constant time operations *guarantees* expected constant time as long as the function family is five-independent. The result that four-independent families do not have this property only shows that *some* four-independent families do not guarantee constant time operations. Some families can have $k < 5$ and

[2] Bradford, PG. and Katehakis, MN. *A Probabilistic Study on Combinatorial Expanders and Hashing.* SIAM J. Comput. (2007) 317(1) pp. 83-111.

[3] Pagh, A., Pagh, R. and Ruzic, M. *Linear Probing with 5-wise Independence.* SIAM Rev. (2011) 53(3) pp. 547-558.

[4] Patrashcu, M. and Thorup, M. *On the k-Independence Required by Linear Probing and Minwise Independence.* ACM Transactions on Algorithms (2016) 12(1) pp. 1-27.

still give expected constant time operations. For example, three-independent *tabulation hashing* does.[5] I cover tabulation hashing later in this chapter.

Constructing Universal Families

All the probabilistic properties you get from universal hashing are only of interest if you can create function families with these properties, and preferably functions that are fast to evaluate. You can do this in multiple ways.

Nearly Universal Families

For constant time operations in chained hashing, nearly universal functions suffice. Dietzfelbinger *et al.*[6] showed that if $N = 2^p$ and $m = 2^q$, $q < p$, then the family of functions

$$h_a(x) = \left(ax \mod 2^p \right) / 2^{p-q}$$

is nearly universal if a is a random odd number $0 < a < 2^p$. They showed that

$$\Pr\left(h_a(x_1) = h_a(x_2) \right) \le 1 / 2^{q-1} = 1 / 2^q.$$

You need one multiplication, ax, one mask $ax \mod 2^p$ and one shift 2^{p-q} to compute this function. If p is the number of bits in a computer

---

[5] Patrashcu, M and Thorup, M. *The Power of Simple Tabulation Hashing.* J. ACM (2012) 59(3) pp. 14:1-14:50.

[6] Dietzfelbinger, M; Hagerup, T; Katajainen, J; and Penttonen, M. *A reliable randomized algorithm for the closest-pair problem*, Journal of Algorithms (1997) 25(1) pp. 19-51.

word, then $ax \quad \text{mod} 2^p$ is just one multiplication in p-bit words, since these are multiplication modulo 2^p, and then you even avoid masking.

Polynomial Construction for *k*-Independent Families

A common way of creating k-independent hash functions, for any k, is based on $k-1$ order polynomials.[7] The construction works as follows: pick a prime, $p > m$. You can pick this prime to be larger than any m you expect to use in your application. Keep it fixed for the algorithm where you use your table. To sample a function, you pick k random integers in $[p]$; call them $a_0, ..., a_{k-1}$. Your function is

$$h(x) = \left(\sum_{i=1}^{k-1} a_i x^i \right) \quad \text{mod } p \text{ mod } m$$

Allocating the data you need to represent a polynomial hash function is trivial. If you use 32-bit numbers it is simple as this:

```
malloc(sizeof(uint32_t) * k);
```

Once you allocate the memory, you can sample functions by picking k random numbers and putting them in this array:

```
void poly_sample(uint32_t *a, int k, uint32_t p)
{
    for (int i = 0; i < k; ++i) {
        a[i] = rand() % p;
    }
}
```

---

[7] Wegman MN. and Carter JL. *New hash functions and their use in authentication and set equality.* Journal of Computer and System Sciences (1981) 22(3) pp. 265-279.

Here, I am assuming that you do the mapping into m bins as a separate operation. The mapping will be the same for all hash functions, so it is not specific to universal hashing.

For Mersenne primes, primes of the form $2^l - 1$, you can avoid the modulo operation and replace it with hashing and shifting, as mentioned in Chapter 2.

```
uint64_t
mod_Mersenne(uint64_t x, uint8_t s)
{
    uint64_t p = (uint64_t)(1 << s) - 1;
    uint64_t y = (x & p) + (x >> s);
    return (y > p) ? y - p : y;
}

uint32_t
poly_hash2_Mersenne(uint32_t x, uint32_t *a, uint8_t s)
{
    uint64_t ax1 = mod_Mersenne((uint64_t)a[1] *
    (uint64_t)x, s);
    uint32_t y = (uint32_t) mod_Mersenne(a[0] + ax1, s);
    return y;
}

uint32_t
poly_hash5_Mersenne(uint32_t x, uint32_t *a, uint8_t s)
{
    // No need for % p for the first value, it will fit
    // in 64-bit.
    uint64_t x1 = (uint64_t)x;
    uint64_t x2 = mod_Mersenne(x1 * (uint64_t)x, s);
    uint64_t x3 = mod_Mersenne(x2 * (uint64_t)x, s);
    uint64_t x4 = mod_Mersenne(x3 * (uint64_t)x, s);
```

```
uint64_t a0 = (uint64_t)a[0];
uint64_t ax1 = (uint64_t)a[1] * x1;
uint64_t ax2 = (uint64_t)a[2] * x2;
uint64_t ax3 = (uint64_t)a[3] * x3;
uint64_t ax4 = (uint64_t)a[4] * x4;

// Since all values fit in 32 bits we
// can add them in 64 bits without overflow
uint64_t y = a0 + ax1 + ax2 + ax3 + ax4;
return (uint32_t)mod_Mersenne(y, s);
}
```

For 32-bit words, you need to do multiplication in 64-bit words, and you need the modulo after each operation to keep them in 64-bit words.

Tabulation Hashing

Tabulation hashing[8] is another way to construct a universal family. Tabulation hashing only gives you three-independence, but it still gives you expected constant time operations for linear probing.

Tabulation hashing uses a table and has more initialization overhead than the polynomial construction, but it compensates for this with faster evaluation times. It avoids expensive multiplication and modulus operations and replaces them with table lookups and XOR operations.

Tabulation hashing maps p-bit words ($N = 2^p$) to q-bit words ($m = 2^q$) by splitting application keys into r-bit chunks; there are $t = p/r$ of these. You now build a table T with one row for each of the t chunks and 2^r columns. In each of the cells of T, you put a random q-bit number.

For the key x, let x_0 denote the first r bits in x, x_1 the next r bits, and so on until x_{t-1}. Because each of the x_i r-bit chunks can be used to index into

---

[8] Carter JL an Wegman MN. *Universal classes of hash functions*. Journal of Computer and System Sciences (1979) 18(2) pp. 143-154.

an array of length 2^r you can get a q-bit word from $T[i, x_i]$ for each $i = 0, \ldots,$ $t - 1$. You then XOR these together to get the hash key:

$$h(x) = T[0, x_0] \oplus T[1, x_1] \oplus \cdots \oplus T[t-1, x_{t-1}]$$

The 2^r number of columns might scare you—exponential numbers always should—but you work with small r values, which keeps the problem under control.

Indexing into q-bit words requires a lot of bit-fiddling, but if you stick to the number of bits available as C data types, you can handle it by casting a pointer, as you will see shortly.

You can treat all tables as bytes when you allocate them. You need to pick an r value. That also defines $t = p/r$ (I assume that p is always 32). Then, for q, you can pick 8-, 16-, and 32-bit words, corresponding to uint8_t, uint16_t, and uint32_t.

For example, for $r = 2$ and $q = 16$ (i.e. uint16_t), you allocate like this:

```
int p = 32;
int r = 2;
int q = 16;
int no_cols = (1 << r);
int t = p / r;
no_cols = (1 << r);
bytes = t * no_cols * q / 8;
uint8_t *T8 = malloc(bytes);
```

I called the table T8 to indicate that it contains bytes, uint8_t. You always allocate a byte array, but you will cast it to different types for different q.

You can treat the table as an array of 32-bit words and sample it like this:

```
void tabulation_sample(uint32_t *start, uint32_t *end)
{
    while (start != end)
        *(start++) = rand();
}
```

Once the byte-array is allocated, you cast it to 32-bit numbers and sample into it:

```
int32_t *T32 = (uint32_t*)T8;
int32_t *T32_end = (uint32_t*)(T8 + bytes);
tabulation_sample(T32, T32_end);
```

A straightforward approach to hashing numbers, for example 32-bit numbers using uint32_t, would be this:

```
uint32_t
tabulation_hash(uint32_t x, uint32_t *T, int p, int r)
{
    int t = p / r;
    int no_cols = 1 << r;
    uint32_t r_mask = (1 << r) - 1;

    uint32_t y = 0;
    for (int i = 0; i < t; ++i) {
        y ^= T[i * no_cols + (x & r_mask)];
        x >>= r;
    }

    return y;
}
```

This, however, involves multiplications to compute the indices into T, and more than for the polynomial function for most choices of r. You can also, however, fix the indices at compile time if you use a specialized function for each r and q combination. Hashing an $r = 8$ table with $q = 16$ would look like this:

```
uint32_t
tabulation_hash_r8_q16(uint32_t x, uint8_t *T)
{
    //These are all known at compile time
    const int r = 8;
    const uint32_t no_cols = 1 << r;
    const uint32_t mask = (1 << r) - 1;

    // q == 16
    uint16_t *T_ = (uint16_t*)T;
    // r == 8 -> t == 4
    uint32_t y;
    y  = T_[0 * no_cols + (x & mask)]; x >>= r;
    y ^= T_[1 * no_cols + (x & mask)]; x >>= r;
    y ^= T_[2 * no_cols + (x & mask)]; x >>= r;
    y ^= T_[3 * no_cols + (x & mask)];

    return y;
}
```

I unrolled the loop here to gain more speed.

Different choices of r will have different tradeoffs, but you can specialize functions to any given application or, based on experiments, pick an r that is generally good. If you know what q values you are going to need, you can also fix that. The easiest, however, is to use 32-bit numbers. It will make the tables larger than for smaller q, and the initialization correspondently slower, but you will never use an m larger than q^{32}, so it will always work.

You could also adjust the function as the table grows to larger m, but that would require calling the hash function through a pointer, and computing jump points like that can confuse the CPUs pipelining and slow down the hashing.

Performance Comparison

In Figure 7-1, I plotted the cost of sampling functions both for polynomials and tabulation hashing. I normalized the time measurements by dividing by the mean of the degree two polynomial computation, which is the fastest. That way, each of the other times is relative to that and shows how much slower they are. The mean times are these:

Function	Time
Polynomial k=2	1.00
Polynomial k=5	1.99
Tabulation r=2 q=8	4.45
Tabulation r=2 q=16	8.75
Tabulation r=2 q=32	17.55
Tabulation r=4 q=8	8.76
Tabulation r=4 q=16	18.27
Tabulation r=4 q=32	38.01
Tabulation r=8 q=8	76.18
Tabulation r=8 q=16	150.40
Tabulation r=8 q=32	296.41

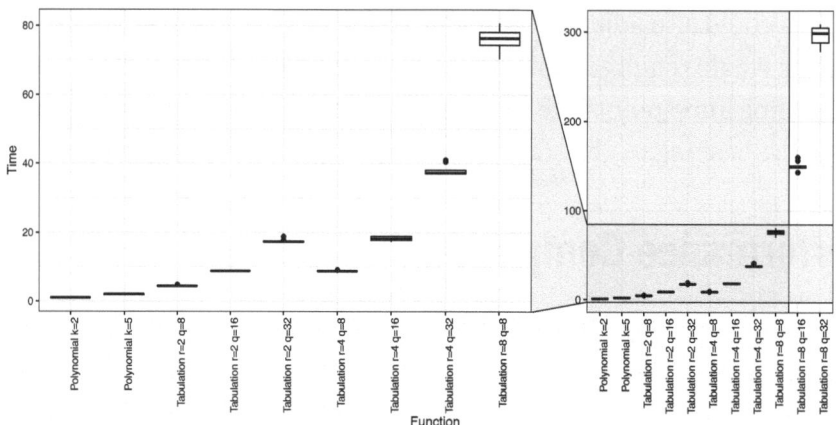

Figure 7-1. *Initialization performance relative to sampling two random integers (polynomial with $k=2$)*

There is a larger overhead in filling the tables compared to sample coefficients for the polynomials, and for large r, where the 2^r columns in the table are problematic, this is substantial. If you stick with $q = 32$, to get a value that will work for all choices of m, you have 20 to 40 times the allocation cost. This needs to be compensated for by the speed of the hash functions. Luckily, tabulation hashing is *much* faster than computing polynomials.

Figure 7-2 shows a comparison of the functions, normalized with the performance of tabulation with $p = 16$ and $r = 8$. The following table shows the mean of the measurements. The tabulation hash functions are an order of magnitude faster than the degree two polynomial and twice as fast at the Mersenne prime degree two function. For the degree five polynomial, necessary for constant time linear probing, the tabulation functions are four times as fast.

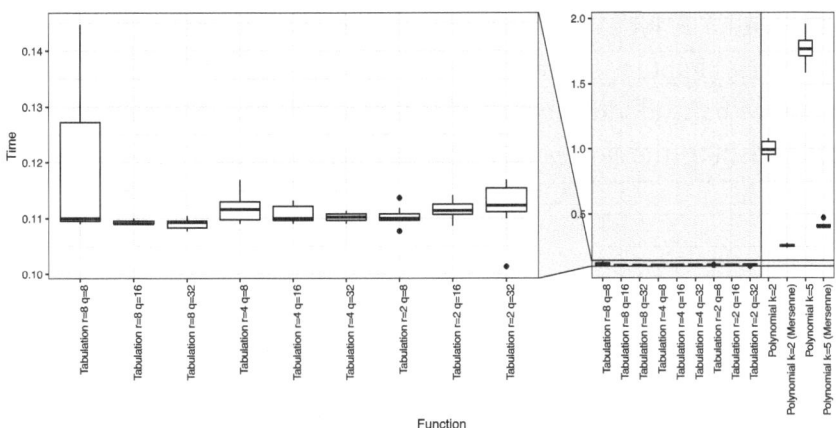

Figure 7-2. *Hashing performance relative to the degree two polynomial computation*

Function	Mean
Tabulation r=8 q=8	0.118
Tabulation r=8 q=16	0.109
Tabulation r=8 q=32	0.109
Tabulation r=4 q=8	0.112
Tabulation r=4 q=16	0.111
Tabulation r=4 q=32	0.110
Tabulation r=2 q=8	0.110
Tabulation r=2 q=16	0.111
Tabulation r=2 q=32	0.112
Polynomial k=2	1.00
Polynomial k=2 (Mersenne)	0.259
Polynomial k=5	1.78
Polynomial k=5 (Mersenne)	0.414

In Figure 7-3, for comparison with the heuristic hash functions from the previous chapter, I show the $q = 32$ bit tables and the polynomials together with the identity function—a baseline that does nothing—and the Jenkins hashing, the slowest from the previous chapter.

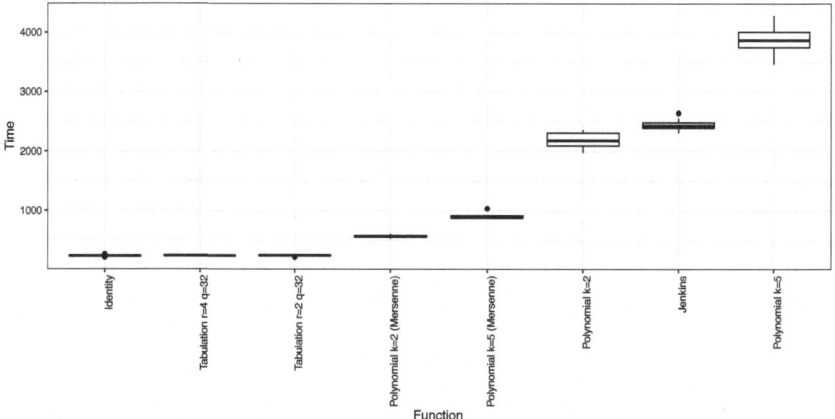

Figure 7-3. *Heuristic hash functions vs universal hash functions*

It is clear that the universal hashing functions are competitive as long as you use Mersenne primes for the polynomials. They are faster to compute than the Jenkins hashing while providing stronger probabilistic guarantees.

With the large initialization cost for tabulation hashing but faster hashing operations, you should consider how many operations you need to do before tabulation hashing outperforms the polynomial method. I plotted this in Figure 7-4. Again, the time measures are relative—I normalized them by the initialization cost for the degree two polynomial. If you do not re-hash more often than about every 100th operation, the tabulation hashing is generally faster than the polynomial.

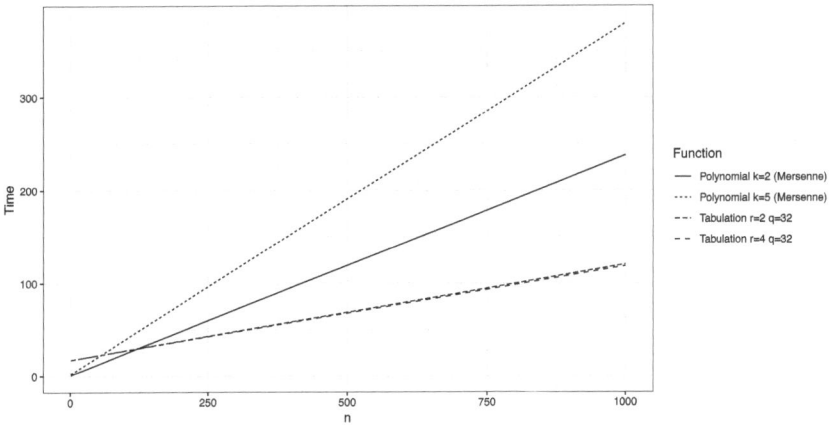

Figure 7-4. *Method performance as a function of n*

Re-hashing

Having guarantees on the expected running times does not mean that you have guarantees for any specific choice of hash function that you sampled, of course. You only get the average behavior over many samples. One technique for getting average behavior is to resample from time to time. If you do this, one unlucky sample will only affect some operations and will, with high probability, be replaced by a better choice when you resample.

You cannot re-hash too often since re-hashing is a linear time operation—you need to move all the keys from the bins where the old hash function mapped them, and to the bins where the new hash function is assigning them. If you do not frequently re-hash, though, you do not get the average behavior.

If you rehash every time you spend some $O(n)$ time on hash table operations, then you have amortized the cost of re-hashing. What factor you will multiply to n for this depends on the hash function sampling and the cost of moving keys. You can experiment to find a good value for your choices.

To see an example of using re-hashing, let's go back to the resizing tables in Chapter 4 and use the open addressing conflict resolution. You also need to add user keys, but not as general as in Chapter 5; in this case, the example assumes that you have user keys that you hash to get bin indices.

First, define a family of hash functions from which you can sample hash functions. I use a $r = 4$, $q = 32$ tabular hash function.

```
#define R 4
#define Q 32
#define HASH_FUNC_WORDS (Q * (1 << R) / sizeof(uint32_t))

typedef uint32_t hash_func[HASH_FUNC_WORDS];

// Sample a new function and place it in f
void tabulation_sample(hash_func f) {
  uint32_t *start = f;
  uint32_t *end = start + HASH_FUNC_WORDS;
  while (start != end)
    *(start++) = rand();
}

// tabulation hashing, r=4, q=32
uint32_t hash(uint32_t x, hash_func f) {
  const uint32_t no_cols = 1 << R;
  const uint32_t mask = no_cols - 1;

  uint32_t y = 0;
  y ^= f[0 * no_cols + (x & mask)]; x >>= R;
  y ^= f[1 * no_cols + (x & mask)]; x >>= R;
  y ^= f[2 * no_cols + (x & mask)]; x >>= R;
  y ^= f[3 * no_cols + (x & mask)]; x >>= R;
  y ^= f[4 * no_cols + (x & mask)]; x >>= R;
  y ^= f[5 * no_cols + (x & mask)]; x >>= R;
```

```
y ^= f[6 * no_cols + (x & mask)]; x >>= R;
y ^= f[7 * no_cols + (x & mask)];

return y;
}
```

With a hash_func, you can sample a new function using tabulation_
sample() and map a user key into a hash key using hash().

For the hash table, you place user keys in the bins—those are the ones
you need to match to have a hit, not the hashed keys—and in the table, you
place a hash_func and a counter of how many operations you have done
since the last re-hash.

```
struct bin {
  unsigned int user_key; // User (not hash) key
  int in_probe : 1;
  int is_empty : 1;
};

struct hash_table {
  struct bin *bins;
  unsigned int size;
  unsigned int used;
  unsigned int active;

  // sampled hash function
  hash_func hash_func;
  // counter to check if it is time to re-hash
  unsigned int ops_since_rehash;
};
```

You can use any probing strategy with the table, but I use the simple linear probe:

```
unsigned int static
p(unsigned int k, unsigned int i, unsigned int m)
{
  return (k + i) & (m - 1);
}
```

Creating and deleting tables involves the same functions as in Chapter 4:

```
struct hash_table *new_table() {
  struct hash_table *table = malloc(sizeof *table);
  init_table(table, MIN_SIZE, NULL, NULL);
  return table;
}

void delete_table(struct hash_table *table) {
  free(table->bins);
  free(table);
}
```

But in init_table(), you add a call to tabulation_sample() to get new hash functions any time you create a new table, resize a table, or re-hash.[9]

```
static void init_table(struct hash_table *table, unsigned
int size,
                  struct bin *begin, struct bin *end) {
  // Initialize table members
```

---

[9] This example also uses table->attribute = value instead of the (struct hash_table){attributes} expressions, so you don't have to copy the hash_func, but this is a minor change.

```
  table->bins = malloc(size * sizeof *table->bins);
  table->size = size;
  table->used = 0;
  table->active = 0;
  table->ops_since_rehash = 0;

  // Initialize the hash table with a new function
  // from the hash family
  tabulation_sample(table->hash_func);

  // Initialize bins
  struct bin empty_bin = {.in_probe = false, .is_empty = true};
  for (unsigned int i = 0; i < table->size; i++) {
    table->bins[i] = empty_bin;
  }

  // Copy the old bins to the new table
  for (struct bin *bin = begin; bin != end; bin++) {
    if (!bin->is_empty) {
      insert_key(table, bin->user_key);
    }
  }
}
```

As in Chapter 4, resizing is mostly handled by init_table(), except for extracting the old bins before calling the initialization code, and because resizing handles mapping the old bins to the new one, you can implement re-hashing as a resize (it doesn't change the size of the table).

```
static void
resize(struct hash_table *table, unsigned int new_size)
{
  //Remember the old bins until we have moved them.
  struct bin *old_bins_begin = table->bins,
             *old_bins_end = old_bins_begin + table->size;
```

```
  // Update the table and copy the old active bins to it.
  init_table(table, new_size, old_bins_begin, old_bins_end);

  // Finally, free memory for old bins
  free(old_bins_begin);
}

static void
rehash(struct hash_table *table)
{
  // Resizing and re-hashing is the same code,
  // except we don't change the size.
  resize(table, table->size);
}
```

Because you now work with the user and hash keys, you have to update the search functions. You have found a key if you have found the user key, not just the hash key (since you could have collisions). You need to use the hash key for the probe but the user key to check if a key is in the current bin. Aside from that, the functions are the same as in Chapter 4:

```
// Find the bin containing key or the first bin
// past the end of its probe
struct bin *
find_key(struct hash_table *table,
         unsigned int user_key,
         uint32_t hash_key)
{
  for (unsigned int i = 0; i < table->size; i++) {
    struct bin *bin = table->bins + p(hash_key, i,
table->size);
    if (bin->user_key == user_key || !bin->in_probe)
      return bin;
  }
```

```
  // The table is full. This should not happen!
  assert(false);
}

// Find the first empty bin in its probe.
struct bin *
find_empty(struct hash_table *table, uint32_t hash_key)
{
  for (unsigned int i = 0; i < table->size; i++) {
    struct bin *bin = table->bins + p(hash_key, i,
table->size);
    if (bin->is_empty)
      return bin;
  }
  // The table is full. This should not happen!
  assert(false);
}
```

For the three main operations, you need to make two changes. You need to hash the user key to get a hash key and you need to check if you have performed table->size operations since the last re-hash. If you have, you need to call rehash().

```
void
insert_key(struct hash_table *table, unsigned int user_key)
{
  if (table->ops_since_rehash++ > table->size)
    rehash(table);

  uint32_t hash_key = hash(user_key, table->hash_func);
  struct bin *bin = find_key(table, user_key, hash_key);

  if (bin->user_key != user_key || bin->is_empty) {
    struct bin *key_bin = find_empty(table, hash_key);
```

```
      table->active++;
      if (!key_bin->in_probe)
        table->used++; // We are using a new bin

      *key_bin =
          (struct bin){.in_probe = true,
                       .is_empty = false,
                       .user_key = user_key};

      if (table->used > table->size / 2)
        resize(table, table->size * 2);
    }
  }
}
bool
contains_key(struct hash_table *table, unsigned int user_key)
{
  if (table->ops_since_rehash++ > table->size)
    rehash(table);

  uint32_t hash_key = hash(user_key, table->hash_func);
  struct bin *bin = find_key(table, user_key, hash_key);
  return bin->user_key == user_key && !bin->is_empty;
}

void
delete_key(struct hash_table *table, unsigned int user_key)
{
  if (table->ops_since_rehash++ > table->size)
    rehash(table);

  uint32_t hash_key = hash(user_key, table->hash_func);
  struct bin *bin = find_key(table, user_key, hash_key);
  if (bin->user_key != user_key)
    return; // Nothing more to do
```

```
  bin->is_empty = true;
  table->active--;

  if (table->active < table->size / 8
      && table->size > MIN_SIZE)
    resize(table, table->size / 2);
}
```

CHAPTER 8

Conclusions

This book explored the hash table data structure. It covered how to map keys from a large space—whereby you assume that the keys are uniformly distributed—into a small space of table bins. It considered a table's performance as a function of the number of bins versus how many keys are stored in a table. It also considered a table's performance as a function of the number of bins versus how many keys are stored in a table. This book covered strategies for handling collisions when two or more different keys map to the same bin and the performance consequences of the choice of strategy. It also discussed how to dynamically adjust the size of tables to avoid having them fill up and incurring high runtime performance penalties as a consequence, while ensuring that you do not allocate tables larger than necessary and incur memory penalties as a consequence.

It is risky to assume that keys are uniformly distributed before you map them to bins, and for natural keys in most applications, where keys might be strings or numbers, this is not true. Generally, it is necessary to first map the application keys to a uniformly distributed space of keys before you can use these "random" keys in a hash table. In the literature, hash functions are often considered functions that map application keys to bins. I considered this mapping process having two or three separate steps in this book. The first step is application-dependent and reduces your data to a number. The (optional) second step scrambles the keys, bringing them closer to being uniformly distributed. The last step then maps the hash keys to bins. I referred to the first two steps as hash functions but not the third.

© The Editor(s) (if applicable) and The Author(s),
under exclusive license to APress Media, LLC, part of Springer Nature 2024
T. Mailund, *The Joys of Hashing*, https://doi.org/10.1007/979-8-8688-0826-5_8

Constructing hash functions that create close to uniformly distributed hash keys is a research field in its own right and an essential part of modern cryptography research, but it's also beyond the scope of this book. Here, I chose to focus mainly on the hash table data structure and covered a few functions for scrambling application hash functions.

There is much more to hashing and hash tables than I have managed to cover in this book. But now that you know the basics, you should be able to implement your own tables, and from there, read and understand research papers about more advanced topics. I wish you the best of luck in your future relationship with hashing.

Index

A

Adding keys, 130
Additive hashing function,
    157–158, 160, 161, 179
add_map() function, 147
add_map_internal() function,
    140, 142, 147
allocated_subtables variable,
    103, 107, 113
Amortized operation cost, 96, 97
Amortized resizing costs
    abstract interface of stack, 62
    array to another, 67
    banking analogy, 69
    computations, 66
    constant factor, 65
    deletion, 70
    doubling the size, 66
    growable array, 62, 63
    load factor, 69
    minimum size, 70
    n operations, 62
    pops, 68
    realloc(), 65
    running time, 62, 67, 68
    runtime analysis, 69
    stack

abstract interface, 63
    creating and deleting, 63
    pushing and popping, 64
    sufficiently low, 68
    time depends, 62
Application keys, 1, 115–117,
    186–188
assert(), 76
assert(false) statement, 145

B

Banking analogy, 69
Big-endian and small-endian
    architectures, 159
Bin index, 2, 3, 89, 99, 100, 104, 106
Bit-masking, 89, 97, 108
Bit-operations, 18

C

Callback functions, 116, 117
Chained hashing, 35–37, 47, 57–59,
    102, 127, 189, 190
Chained hashing table, 47, 119
Chained hash tables, 70–74, 186
Chaining, linked lists, 30–35
Code-generating macros, 126, 133

Colliding keys, 29, 43
Collision resolution
    constant time operations, 189
    functions, 189
    linear probing, 189
    methods, 54
    tabulation hashing, 190
Collisions, 6, 22, 29, 48
Conflict resolution methods, 57
Constructing universal families
    probabilistic properties, 190
contains_key, 42, 74
copy_key function, 138
copy_links function, 132
copy_val function, 138

D, E

DELETE_LINK macro, 125, 126
Deleting keys, 20, 38, 130
Double hashing, 43–45, 48, 50,
    54–56, 58, 97, 98, 102
Dynamic resizing
    allocated_subtables variable,
        107, 113
    bin index, 100, 104, 106
    bit operations, 99
    eight bits, 100
    growing and shrinking, 99, 101
    indexing keys, 100
    linear hashing, 99
    merge operation, 108
    merging bins, 113
    number of bits, 103
    pairs of bins to split and
        merge, 102
    split, 101
    split bin, 102, 111
    split operation, 108
    structure, 103
    sub-tables, 99, 100, 102, 106,
        107, 113
    table->table_bits, 109
    table->tables array, 109

F

find_empty() function, 42
find_key() function, 41, 42,
    146, 148
for loop, 145
free_bin() function, 143, 146
FREE_KEY, 124–126
free_key function, 138
free_list() function, 32, 129
free_val function, 138

G

Generic programming, 118
Generics, 118, 119, 133, 150
GEN_LIST_ADD_KEY macro,
    123, 124
GEN_LIST_FREE_LIST
    macro, 125
get_bin() function, 147, 148
get_key_bin, 130
Growable array, 62, 63

H

HASH_FN, 128
Hash functions, 138, 153, 154, 167,
        172, 179, 197, 202, 211, 212
    computation, 154
    guarantees, 154
    properties, 153
    randomization, 154
    randomization tricks, 154
    signature, 175
Hashing, 3, 48, 157–162, 179, 180, 199
Hashing computer words
    consecutive numbers, 155
    data structures, 155
    functions, 157
    hash function, 155
    multiple-word, 156
    parameter, 156
    single-word, 156
    XOR, 156
Hashing strings, bytes
    functions, 176
    variable length, 175
Hash key collisions, 21
Hash keys, 1, 115, 116
    add bit, 8
    allocation error, 13
    array, 8
    collision, 22, 26
    flexible array, 14
    indices, 14
    initialization, 11
    memory alignment, 9

primes, 16
space, 9
uniform distribution, 23
variant, 10
hash(K key), 118
Hash maps, 134
    addition and deletion, 146–149
    creation and resizing
        processes, 140–142
    definition, 137–139
    freeing tables, 142, 143
    hash tables, 135
    key and value types, 136, 137
    lookup_key() function, 145–147
    void pointer, 134
HASH_NAME, 128
Hash table operations, 18–21, 90, 201
Hash tables, 29, 35, 38–40, 46–49,
        59, 115, 117, 119, 128, 134,
        135, 151
    application maps, 5
    primary responsibility, 4
    second responsibility, 4
    set and map data structure, 115
Hash values, 136, 137, 140, 144, 150
Helper functions, 40, 76, 138
Heuristic hash functions, 151, 200
HTABLE(HASH_NAME), 128

I

Index bins, 16
init_table() function, 75, 78, 79,
        140, 142, 204, 205

in_probe flag, 39, 149
insert_key(), 79
is_active_bin, 139
is_active_bin() helper function, 143
is_empty flag, 39, 149
IS_EQ, 125, 126
ITR_END macro, 122
ITR(LIST) macro, 122

LIST_NAME##_free_list
    function, 125
Load factors, 46, 80–84, 86, 88, 89
   probes for different load
    factors, 51
   probes for different small load
    factors, 52
lookup_key() function, 145

J

jenkins_hash function, 175, 177
Jenkins hashing, 171, 180, 200
Jenkins' lookup2 hash function,
    173, 174
Jenkins' lookup2 hashing, 174

M

malloc() errors, 12
Mersenne prime degree, 198
Mersenne primes, 17, 192, 200
Micro-optimisations, 17
Modulo operator, 14

K

KE_TYPE, 119
KEY_TYPE, 124
key_type function, 137

N

Non-empty bin, 79

O

One-at-a-time function, 172
One-at-a-time hash function,
    163, 164, 168–170
One-at-a-time hashing, 165–169,
    171, 180
OOP techniques, 118
Open addressing, 38
   collision resolution, 55
   find_key() function, 41, 42
   hashing, 48–54
   hash tables, 74–80

L

Linear hashing, 45, 99
Linear probing, 42, 43, 48, 50, 54,
    56–58, 97
link structure, 120
Linked list operations, 31
Link's next pointer, 30, 31
*list, 33
LIST_FN, 128
LIST_NAME, 119, 124

in_probe flag, 39
is_free, 39
is_empty flag, 39
probing, 38
probing strategy, 42–44

P, Q

Polynomial computation, 197, 199
Polynomial function, 196
Polynomial hash function, 191
Pop operation, 68
Prime-number-sized hash
    tables, 153
Probe lengths, mean *vs.*
    theoretical, 53
Probing, 38, 40, 42–44, 138
Probing strategy p(k,i), 38
PUSH_NEW_LINK macro, 123

R

Randomized algorithms, 181
Re-hashing, 201–209
Resizing
    amortizing resizing
        costs, 62–70
    chained hash tables, 70–74
    cost of resizing *vs.* the cost of
        probing, 88
    dynamic, 99–114
    experiments, 84–89
    hash table, 61
    load factor, 61, 80–83

open addressing hash
    tables, 74–80
powers of two
    allocation cost, 94
    amortized operation
        cost, 96, 97
    analytical result, 93
    and binning, 97
    components of running
        time, 95
    components of time
        usage, 92, 93
    double hashing, 98
    growing array, 91, 92
    linear cost per insertion
        operation, 94
    modulo, 89
    optimal value, 96
    parameter, 89
    primes, 90
    running time for
        rescaling, 92, 93
    time performance for tables
        of prime size, 98
    thresholds, 87
Resolution strategies, 46, 84, 189–190
Rotate operation, 159
Rotating hashing, 159–162, 179
Rotation hash function, 161

S

Smoothed data, 86, 87
Square approximation, 27

stack structure, 63
store_in_bin()function, 148
strcmp(), 127
struct link, 31, 32
struct link **, 35
struct my_type_list, 121
SUBTABLE_BITS
     variable, 103
Sub-tables, 99, 102, 106, 107

T

table_bits variable, 103
table->table_bits, 109
table->tables array, 109
Tabulation functions, 198
Tabulation hashing, 193–198
tabulation_sample(), 204
Theoretical probe
     length, 49, 53
Time usage measurements, 86
typeof() operator, 122
Type-specific tables, 118

U

Universal functions, 187, 190
Universal hashing
    chained, 184
    collisions, 188
    constant time operations, 186
    family, 186
    function, 183
    independent families, 187
    keys, 187
    operations, 184, 186
    pairwise independent, 187
    probability theory, 183
    straightforward approach, 195
    table, 184
    universal, 185

V, W, X, Y, Z

value_type function, 137
void * const, 146
void * objects, 134
void * types, 134